T0360866

Qualitative Management Research in Context

This concise book uses narrative fiction to address how researchers can conduct qualitative research using both online and first-hand data and digital and face-to-face methods.

The book is structured around four phases of the research process – accessing management field research, writing the literature review, collecting and analysing data and enacting qualitative research and finally the creative process of writing qualitative research. Theory and practice are merged through a situation-based case study within each chapter, with the methods and tools employed in each context explored through narrative fiction. The protagonists of each case have specific questions, emotions and ambiguities that qualitative researchers need to face, offering a unique approach to the practice of qualitative research and how it is used in real-life situations.

Founded on the idea of enacting and not just doing qualitative research, this book offers toolkits that the researcher can use to operationalise research from start to finish. It will be of interest to postgraduate students conducting research-based projects in business and management, researchers and academics looking for a fresh approach.

Bruno Luiz Américo has a Ph.D. in Management from the Federal University of Espírito Santo, Brazil.

Stewart Clegg is Professor in the School of Project Management and the John Grill Institute of Project Leadership at the University of Sydney, Australia. In addition, he holds Visiting Professorship at the University of Stavanger Business School, Norway; the University of Johannesburg Business School, South Africa and Nova School of Business and Economics, Carcavelos, Portugal. He is an Emeritus Professor at the University of Technology, Sydney.

César Tureta is Professor of Organization Studies at the Federal University of Espírito Santo, Brazil.

Routledge Focus on Business and Management

The fields of business and management have grown exponentially as areas of research and education. This growth presents challenges for readers trying to keep up with the latest important insights. *Routledge Focus on Business and Management* presents small books on big topics and how they intersect with the world of business research.

Individually, each title in the series provides coverage of a key academic topic, whilst collectively, the series forms a comprehensive collection across the business disciplines.

Organizations and Complex Adaptive Systems
Masha Fidanboy

Managing Complexity in Healthcare
Lesley Kuhn and Kieran Le Plastrier

Work Organizational Reforms and Employment Relations in the Automotive Industry
American Employment Relations in Transition
Kenichi Shinohara

Qualitative Management Research in Context
Data Collection, Interpretation and Narrative
Bruno Luiz Américo, Stewart Clegg and César Tureta (eds)

Marx in Management and Organisation Studies
Rethinking Value, Labour and Class Struggles
Frederick Harry Pitts

For more information about this series, please visit: www.routledge.com/Routledge-Focus-on-Business-and-Management/book-series/FBM

Qualitative Management Research in Context

Data Collection, Interpretation and Narrative

**Edited by Bruno Luiz Américo,
Stewart Clegg and César Tureta**

Routledge
Taylor & Francis Group

LONDON AND NEW YORK

First published 2023
by Routledge
4 Park Square, Milton Park, Abingdon, Oxon OX14 4RN

and by Routledge
605 Third Avenue, New York, NY 10158

Routledge is an imprint of the Taylor & Francis Group, an informa business

British Library Cataloguing-in-Publication Data
A catalogue record for this book is available from the British Library

Library of Congress Cataloging-in-Publication Data
Names: Américo, Bruno Luiz, editor. | Clegg, Stewart, editor. |
Tureta, César, editor.
Title: Qualitative management research in context : data collection, interpretation and narrative / edited by Bruno Luiz Américo, Stewart Clegg, César Tureta.
Description: Abingdon, Oxon ; New York, NY : Routledge, 2023. |
Includes bibliographical references and index. | Identifiers:
LCCN 2022016785 (print) | LCCN 2022016786 (ebook) |
ISBN 9781032055718 (hardback) | ISBN 9781032055732 (paperback) |
ISBN 9781003198161 (ebook)
Subjects: LCSH: Management–Research–Methodology. |
Qualitative research–Methodology.
Classification: LCC HD30.4 .Q345 2023 (print) | LCC HD30.4 (ebook) |
DDC 650.072/1–dc23/eng/20220427
LC record available at https://lccn.loc.gov/2022016785
LC ebook record available at https://lccn.loc.gov/2022016786

ISBN: 978-1-032-05571-8 (hbk)
ISBN: 978-1-032-05573-2 (pbk)
ISBN: 978-1-003-19816-1 (ebk)

DOI: 10.4324/9781003198161

Typeset in Times New Roman
by Newgen Publishing UK

Contents

Figures

Tables

Contributors

Bruno Luiz Américo has a Ph.D. in Management from the Federal University of Espírito Santo, Brazil.

Fagner Carniel is a professor at the Department of Social Sciences at the State University of Maringá. Brazil.

Stewart Clegg is Professor in the School of Project Management and the John Grill Institute of Project Leadership at the University of Sydney, Australia. In addition, he holds Visiting Professorship at the University of Stavanger Business School, Norway; the University of Johannesburg Business School, South Africa and Nova School of Business and Economics, Carcavelos, Portugal. In addition, he is an Emeritus Professor at the University of Technology, Sydney.

Leticia Dias Fantinel is an adjunct professor of the Department of Administration and the Postgraduate Programme in Administration at the Federal University of Espírito Santo, Brazil.

César Tureta is Professor of Organization Studies at the Federal University of Espírito Santo, Brazil.

Introduction

*Bruno Luiz Américo, Stewart Clegg and
César Tureta*

Keywords: Qualitative research; theorizing; exemplary research.

Expected learning outcomes

At the end of the chapter, readers – students, researchers, early
career or otherwise – will be able to understand the following:

- Changes that have occurred in the past decade in qualitative
  research.
- The complex and multiple social/material/ecological realities
  in which writers, readers and research subjects are immersed.
- How creative writing can be a path to inquiry for theorizing
  and method through qualitative research.
- The importance of ethics in enacting qualitative research.

The challenges of qualitative research: The times they are a-changing

The planetary boundaries (Rockström, 2010; Whiteman, Walker &
Perego, 2013; Heikkurinen, Clegg, Pinnington, Nicolopoulou &
Alcaraz, 2021) for life on the planet are increasingly being challenged.
The second one-in-a-hundred-year flooding in the past year is
occurring in the state in which these words are being written. When
one-in-a-hundred-year floods occur twice in the space of a year, times
certainly are changing. Not only that, the times in which the book
has been written have been marked by a novel coronavirus, causing
COVID-19, which has unleashed major institutional changes in
everyday life. During the COVID-19 pandemic, going to work ceased

DOI: 10.4324/9781003198161-1

to involve travel to an office elsewhere from one's home. Instead, for those whose work can be done remotely, the home became the workplace. Students no longer went to lectures but engaged digitally with their colleagues at their university. Lectures were abandoned and online workshops were adopted.

Online workshops were already replacing the traditional form of the lecture before the pandemic. The tradition of the lecture goes back, historically, to days in which knowledge was not easily available as books were rare and expensive and literacy not widely shared. Those that stood at the lectern dispensed knowledge to their audiences or, if at a pulpit, to their congregations. Institutions, once established, such as the lecture, often persist indefinitely. Sometimes it takes an event that jolts the institution to change it. COVID-19 was such a jolt. Contemporary students ceased to find much value in a lecture that they could 'attend' only remotely. They could probably access the information imparted more easily digitally, at times more convenient rather than when an event was scheduled. The workshop experience is increasingly becoming proactive. Students do and are expected to do things rather than passively receiving a lecture. Universities increasingly provide facilitators to assist students in their inquiries, with the focus shifting more towards students' learning by doing research projects. The cynics might also add that doing this reduces the costs of employing highly qualified and credentialled professors for front-line teaching.

Different research protocols and data collection/analysis instruments, as well as the usual scientific methods, may be required to register these changing times (cf. Buchanan et al., 2007; Hacking, 1992; 1994; Whiteman et al., 2013); hence the title of the section, which refers to Bob Dylan's famous anthem of change. Our book is designed to help students do such projects as might arise from these workshops and to introduce them to some creative ways of enacting qualitative research.

Not only is teaching and learning changing from in person to digital; so is research. Once upon a time the unique aspect of qualitative research was being there. The authenticity of ethnographic research was based on presence. The digital world changes everything. For example, Leeds University Business School recently hosted a public lecture by David Silverman, in which he spoke about doing qualitative research into social distancing in pandemic times.[1] For him, researchers currently face several problems, such as doing fieldwork without a field. He mentioned online interviews and social groups, document research, as well as digital ethnography as solutions to such problems. Accordingly, researchers must not have common assumptions about 'who' must be interviewed; in step with Michel Callon and Lindsay Prior, David

Silverman observes that data (e.g., documents) gained by doing qualitative research into social distancing in pandemic times can and must be analysed in their own right. With Silverman, we focus on qualitative research, a methodology that uses specific data collection methods and analysis to interpret the particularities of the social, material and cultural realities of people's everyday practices and processes. We intend to provide a useful guide to students engaged in workshops doing small qualitative research projects. With Silverman, we take a broad approach to how qualitative research may be done.

Just as individual, professional, group and organizational realities are being transformed due to current global social/environmental crises, such as the COVID-19 pandemic, the methodological paths used by scholarship to interpret events also change constantly. Thus, the methods we use are not neutral tools but are implicated in those empirical events that we investigate (Buchanan & Bryman, 2007; Latour, 2005; Law, 2004; 2009; Majima & Moore, 2009; Whiteman, 2010). Since different methods reflect realities viewed through specific interpretive lenses, rather than specifically describing a reality that can be captured in its objective qualities (Denzin, 2014; Law, 2004; Richardson, 1994), researchers can take advantage of the wide-open political space in which realities can be enacted (Law, 2004; 2009). However, for this 'space' to be used, researchers need to construct methods that counter the challenges posed by emerging complex problems (see Majima & Moore, 2009).

Qualitative research uses both inductive and abductive approaches. Inductive approaches begin with empirical observations and the search for regularities and variations in these observations. Based on these, theorizing aims to generate insights into the patterns that are constituted by the interpretative devices being used. An abductive approach deploys an inferential process to produce hypotheses and theories based on research evidence that throws up surprises. Both approaches contrast with a deductive approach that begins with a theory, developing hypotheses from that theory and then collecting and analysing data to test those hypotheses. We will not provide advice on deductive variations on survey analysis and quantitative data collection and data mining to test hypotheses drawn from theory. We will develop approaches that enable *you* to develop your skills in theorizing as a practice and a process (Clegg, Cunha & Berti, 2022).

Theorizing, as well as clearly communicating theory and method, comprises a complex practice involving multiple realities. On the one hand, it means working in and across fields of professional theoretical practice and occupational craft; on the other hand, it means engaging these theoretical practices and craft in dialogue with data gathered from situations replete with the emotions and ambiguities of everyday life. An example comes from the *Financial Times* journalist (and anthropologist) Gillian Tett (2021). Writing about the US Federal Reserve's attitudes to the probability of inflation, she notes that the Fed should not rely only on quantitative data about inflation projections but should also consider the emotions of consumers. What will be their attitude to retail price increase? Will such increases be seen as a temporary phenomenon, or will they unleash inflationary demands for further wage increases? How might the Fed know these things? Not through standard economic forecasting or even survey analysis of consumers, she suggests. The Fed would be better off tracking sentiment through discursive analyses of key terms appearing in digital communications in cyberspace; it should tap into the cyber peer groups in which people explore anxieties and fears as well as hopes, dreams and schemes. The Fed should conduct qualitative ethnographic research that uncovers how people perceive inflation, how they talk about it in everyday life and the questions that trouble them as well as those that do not. They should employ researchers that embrace curiosity in designing research and doing fieldwork who, at the same time, need to be able to write stories about the practices analysed, which they can communicate clearly.

We have written this book in such a way that it links up with what is by now a rich research seam of narrative fiction (Jermier, 1985; Rhodes & Brown, 2005); fiction (Czarniawska, 2006, 2008; Savage, Cornelissen & Franck, 2018), creative writing (Vickers, 2011; 2013); autoethnography (Boyle & Perry, 2007; Learmonth & Humphreys, 2012); narrative semi-fiction (Bruce, 2019; Vickers, 2015; Whiteman & Phillips, 2008); ethnographic fiction (Watson, 2000); art and aesthetics (Strati, 2009); imagination (Cornelissen, 2019; Harold, 2003) and audio-visual artistic representations (Warren, 2008). These approaches use both cognition and emotions to theorize and write about emergent theories and develop innovative methods for inquiry into contemporary aspects of everyday life in its socio-materiality. Multiple subjects, objects, practices, discourses and reasonings are involved in everyday life and those sociomaterial phenomena which inhabit it (Castro, 2014; Mol, 2002; Mol & Law, 2002).

What is theorizing, theory and method?

For Cornelissen (2017), theory creates an explanation about 'something', such as sensemaking processes or a particular aspect of everyday life. Theorizing is an artisanal practice that can be thought of as an act of conceptualization (Cornelissen, Höllerer & Seidl, 2021) helping us see how things hang together or to uncover hidden aspects.

Buchanan and Bryman (2007, p. 483) characterize method as a tool shaped by research aims, norms of practice and epistemological concerns as well as "significant characteristics of the field of research". These could entail a combination of organizational, historical, political, ethical, evidential and personal data. Any method, as a research tool, is located "as an integral component of a wider, iterative, coherent research system, influencing the social possibilities of data collection as well as the substantive nature of data collected and the nature and direction of theory development" (Buchanan et al., 2007, p. 483). Thus, the research setting and its salient factors are central for researchers' design of paths for data collection and analysis as well as "the development of theoretical and practical outcomes" (Buchanan et al., 2007, p. 483/4).

The changing practice of researching qualitatively

Stengers (2015) suggests reviving the art of paying attention, which the Greeks called *pharmakon*, to the ambiguity and instability of life and its interpretations. When you pay attention and transmit and translate results for others, you do so through a narrative. There are many things of significance for narrating *pharmakon* to which attention should be paid. First, in constructing their methods, researchers must note that instruments of data collection and analysis are assumed to depend, essentially, on the *epistemes* that build them (Hacking, 1992; 1994; Mol, 2002) as well as factors characterizing the research settings (Buchanan et al. & Bryman, 2007). Narration entails drawing on epistemes to address whatever matter and events are at hand discursively. Discursivity is the essence, if not the totality, of qualitative research. Once upon a time, not so far back in the last century, qualitative research was stigmatized as improper social science; it did not include variables, statistics and numbers. It did not aspire to 'physic envy' (Flyvbjerg, 2001). The times have changed. Qualitative research has been growing in the social sciences as well as in applied social sciences. Google Scholar shows such growth: before 1950, only two results show up containing 'qualitative research' in the title[2]. From 1951 to 2010, there are 6,660 results.[3] And from only 2011 to 2021, there are 9,930 results.[4]

Looking at the field in which we work (organization and management studies), a series of papers called 'From the Editors', published by the *Academy of Management Journal* (AMJ) in 2011, discussed the relevance of qualitative research. Bansal and Corley (2011, p. 233) indicate the positive reception of qualitative methods in the AMJ. According to them, "six of the last eight papers awarded AMJ's 'Best Article Award' were based exclusively on qualitative data". Recently, in a paper published in the same journal, Bansal, Smith and Vaara (2018) note the further growth of qualitative research in top management journals. According to the authors, "as we face more wicked problems in our world, scholars are increasingly adopting qualitative methods to unpack these complex challenges." When confronted with wicked problems that do not have a ready diagnosis, curiosity and creativity are required to proceed. Curiosity guides the exploration of complex and ambiguous events during fieldwork, awakening feelings "of interest in a situation where a potential exists for learning" (Kashdan, Stiksma, Disabato, McKnight, Bekier, Kaji & Lazarus, 2018, p. 130). Creativity is a powerful necessity when solving a problem; with creativity and imagination, new and useful ideas can be generated (Amabile & Pratt, 2016) and the tracks of convention detoured in handling complex contemporary challenges for research. As Bansal et al. (2018, p. 1189) noted, in 2018 the publication of qualitative papers hit an all-time high for the AMJ, albeit comprising only 20 per cent of the submissions. Nonetheless, in a journal widely perceived as an orthodox quantitative-oriented publication, this percentage is significant.

With the growth in the number of investigations and the popularity of qualitative research, challenges abound. After all, "there is no accepted 'boilerplate' for writing" (Pratt, 2009, p. 856) about the practice of researching qualitatively. Since there are no overtly accepted rules in qualitative research, Jarzabkowski, Langley and Nigam (2021) point out that qualitative researchers can work with freedom. However, for these authors (2021, p. 70), such freedom "can generate insecurity and the desire for guidance", available, for instance, in methodological texts published in books, handbooks or articles (cf. Cassell, Cunliffe & Grandy, 2017; Easterby-Smith, Golden-Biddle & Locke, 2008; Miles, Huberman & Saldana, 2014; Mir & Jain, 2017; Silverman, 2020; 2022). Approaches abound, such as Guba and Lincoln's (1985) criteria of trustworthiness in data collection and analysis in naturalistic locations and Gioia, Corley and Hamilton's (2013) approach to codifying data. Beyond structures, for Corley, Bansal and Yu (2021), methodological texts also inscribe protocols, such as the Eisenhardt method, the Gioia method or the Langley strategies for theorizing from processual data, as approaches used to assure readers of qualitative research about the rigorous status and quality of the investigation are being reported.

Corley et al. (2021) and Jarzabkowski et al. (2021) argue that a concern with 'structures' and 'protocols' diminishes the capacity for qualitative researchers to make creative leaps (cf. Langley. 1999). For Jarzabkowski et al. (2021), qualitative researchers need to navigate the tensions between rigour (structures, guidelines for organizing, protocols) and creativity (innovation, imagination, induction) (cf. Lê & Schmid, 2020), while embracing pluralism (cf. Bansal & Corley, 2011; Easterby-Smith et al., 2008) and generativity (Carlsen & Dutton, 2011) in qualitative research. Hence, using just a few orthodox approaches for analysis of qualitative data adds little diversity to qualitative research methods (see Bansal & Corley, 2011; 2018; Gehman, Glaser & Eisenhardt, 2018). Doing this merely promises to replace one quantitative orthodoxy with a qualitative orthodoxy. Notwithstanding this, encouraging diversity in qualitative research does not mean that "anything goes" (Bansal & Corley, 2011, p. 235). Any creative endeavour must meet a set of criteria used to evaluate scholarly products in a specific field (Patriotta & Hirsch, 2016). Furthermore, embracing diversity means being open to new experiences, allowing fieldwork to violate researchers' expectations and produce stories that surprise and inform readers.

In the past, how qualitative research could convince others of the plausibility/defensibility of its conclusions has been questioned (see Gioia et al., 2013, p. 15; Grodal, Anteby & Holm, 2020, p. 1), hinting, perhaps, at a degree of inferiority complex on the part of qualitative researchers, that 'physics envy'. Abandoning envy, several studies sought to improve the quality of qualitative research by searching for new approaches that recognized the increasingly emotional, ambiguous and complex nature of everyday life's practices and processes in present times. For instance, past scholarship has linked up with exemplary publications and seminal authors as a guide for practice (see Américo & Clegg, forthcoming, Anderson, 2006; Anderson & Lemken, 2019; Frost & Stablein, 1992; Humphries and Dyer, 2005; Kor, Mahoney, Siemsen & Tan, 2016; Lerman, Mmbaga & Smith, 2020; Lounsbury & Carberry, 2005; Weick, 2005). Such publications provide direction in "conducting and publishing qualitative research" (Lerman et al., 2020, p. 1).

Frost and Stablein (1992) referred to works that provide direction as 'exemplars'. For Frost and Stablein (1992), demystifying the act of doing exemplary research and publication enacts it as a messier, more imperfect, personal, intriguing, exciting, frustrating, depressing, puzzling, surprising and everyday practice performed not by exceptionally gifted individuals but by 'everyday people'. Successful researchers, they established, were not uniquely gifted but worked diligently and persistently, they sought and received advice widely, acted on this advice with judgement. When responding to this advice formally, replying to reviewers and editors, they did so clearly, explaining what they had done and not done, as well as why. Doing all this implies bringing different forms of reflexivity to bear on scenes being described (Cassell, Radcliffe & Malik, 2020), theories being used (Hardy & Clegg; 1997; Hardy, Phillips & Clegg, 2001; Clegg & Hardy, 2006; Van Marrewijk, Veenswijk & Clegg, 2010) or that are inclusive in their reflexivity by referring to aspects of the researchers' identity in doing the research (Koning & Ooi, 2013). Whatever approach is used, it involves using not only *pharmakon* but also *phronesis* (Clegg, Flyvbjerg & Haugaard, 2014), developing practical wisdom through a dialogue between the practical consciousnesses of those being researched and the theoretical consciousnesses that the researcher can bring to the exercise.

The quest for rigour and quality is promoted through innovation in data analysis; for example, by using active categorization to build theory through qualitative analysis (Grodal et al., 2020). Although the practice of creative discovery and strict coding go hand in hand (Locke, Feldman & Golden-Biddle, 2020), research findings do not result from coding practices alone (Jarzabkowski et al., 2021; Langley, 1999). Qualitative research also strives to show quality and rigour through the combination of traditional and emerging knowledge, science and aesthetics, rigorous writing, the use of literary genres and styles, as well as narrative and ethnographic methods (see Caulley, 2008; Phillips, 1995). The lack of theoretical and methodological innovation for qualitative research to make much impact has been noted (Aguinis, Pierce, Bosco & Muslin, 2009; Alvesson & Sandberg, 2013; Hibbert, Sillince, Diefenbach & Cunliffe, 2014). Perhaps these scholars' memories are too truncated to take in the work of innovative and largely forgotten precursors (Thomas & Znaniecki, 1919; Blumer, 1979; Stanley, 2010), who did make use of such methodological innovation. For instance, Thomas and Znaniecki's study of the transition and translation from being a Polish peasant to becoming an industrial worker in the United States used a great deal of creativity in accessing and using data. Thomas and Znaniecki made use of diaries, autobiographies, photographs and official documents as data, extremely creatively.

Being creative means combining disconnected ideas, concepts and methods into new variations (Shalley & Zhou, 2008). For instance, in recent times Berends and Deken (2021) evaluated different options for composing qualitative process research, arguing for and differentiating three options for writing: being inductive, conceptual or using models. Once such different writing styles are acknowledged, scholarship can deal with the challenge of opting between theoretical interpretation or letting the data speak, testifying to the generativity of qualitative research (see Carlsen & Dutton, 2011).

While qualitative research (cf. Cassell et al., 2017; Easterby-Smith et al., 2008; Miles et al., 2014; Mir & Jain, 2017) and the tensions of quality in qualitative research (cf. Berends & Deken, 2021; Grodal et al., 2020; Jarzabkowski et al., 2021; Locke et al., 2020) are widely discussed in excellent books, articles, chapters and handbooks, the present book focuses less on the many structures, protocols, rigidities and procedures of doing qualitative research in favour of a focus on enacting it.

The changing realities and contexts investigated by qualitative research

Historically, qualitative data collection has privileged participant observation, interviews, recordings, accessing documents and other material artefacts as sources of data. Likewise, such data has traditionally been analysed through ethnographic methods, discourse analysis and coding techniques. If past scholarship previously considered that fieldwork's 'emotional encounters' (e.g. acceptance and rejection of access) involved those between 'researcher, gatekeeper and potential informants' (Peticca-Harris, deGama & Elias, 2016), entailing 'facework' (Goffman, 1955), the context is now more divergent. In post-pandemic organizations, consumers and entrepreneurs, organizations and employees increasingly interact not only in person but also through digital media; hence, face-to-face methods require supplementation (cf. Land & Taylor, 2018; Salmons, 2016).

Attending to wicked problems (Bansal et al., 2018) that pervade everyday lived experience attunes qualitative research scholars to be sensitive to those communities of practice they investigate (see Granek & Nakash, 2016). To this end, we argue that qualitative research needs to explore how subjects interact with policies, rules, materials and natures in specific contexts. Researchers that are guided by curiosity and openness to experiences in collecting and analysing data, rather than to a priori concepts or specific theoretical frameworks that restrict the number of surprising phenomena that can be observed, are conducting research grounded in action, what Glaser and Strauss (1967) termed grounded theory.

How to deal with 'wicked problems'?

Addressing emerging wicked problems (Bansal et al., 2018) helps researchers rethink research designs, fieldwork practices and research training, redirecting academic efforts to enact qualitative research in ways other than planned in the past (cf. Peticca-Harris et al., 2016). Curiosity plays a vital role in dealing with wicked problems, because of the nature of these problems. What makes them 'wicked' is that they deal with social or cultural problem unamenable to easy solution for four reasons: incomplete or contradictory knowledge; the number of people and opinions involved; the large economic burden, as well as the interconnected nature of these problems with other problems. As we argued earlier, researchers should embrace curiosity to explore their creativity in doing qualitative research. Through curiosity, investigators can better deal with the fast changes that organizations face. Kashdan et al. (2018, p. 130) state that:

> Curiosity can be commonly defined as the recognition, pursuit, and desire to explore novel, uncertain, complex, and ambiguous events. There is the feeling of interest in a situation where a potential exists for learning. There is a desire to seek out novel experiences – to see what happens, to find out how one will react, or discover how others react.

Eisenhardt, Graebner and Sonenshein (2016, p. 1113) state that inductive methods "excel in situations for which there is limited theory and on problems without clear answers". The qualitative investigator needs to pay initial attention to how communities of practice problematize topics and issues (Stengers, 2015), only then establishing a dialogue with and contributing to specialized literature through theory development. Research is a two-way conversation with the field being researched and the theoretical fields that the researcher is drawn to through experiences gained in collecting data as well as a result of their predispositions. Fundamentally then, all qualitative research should begin with ethnomethodological inquiry. Ethno-methods are the methods members of settings use for making sense, both procedurally and substantively, of the ways of making sense that characterize specific practices. Literally, ethnomethodology means the practices that people use, their folk methodologies. It is not for nothing that Weick's (1995) work on sensemaking was preceded long before by his encounters with ethnomethodology (Weick, 1969), interpreted through an autopoietic framework.

Another challenge in enacting qualitative research is the role of emotion. Although qualitative methodology textbooks represent technical and specialized knowledge, content considering the emotions and ambiguities involved in the situational process of doing qualitative research is scarce (cf. Lofland, Snow, Anderson & Lofland, 2006; Warren & Karner, 2004). Many books on research methodology, research design and research methods assume the co-presence of researcher(s) and subject(s), but only a few investigations inquire into the emotional ambiguity entailed in both interacting with people's ways of managing their affairs as well as representing how doing so can lead to entanglement in agonistic and symbiotic ways. There are some exceptions, which we will address shortly (cf. Jermier, 1985; Taylor, 2000; Vickers, 2011, 2013, 2015; Whiteman, 2004). Both Whiteman et al. (2009) and Weick (1999; 2002) suggest that emotions and cognitions guide fieldwork and must be used in the research report.

These issues impose challenges that researchers should address. Caulley (2008) demands more creativity in writing qualitative research reports. To write creatively, scholars should let their curiosity and creativity emerge by being 'open to experience' and to the 'experienced world' (Lofland et al., 2006; Weick, 1999; Whiteman et al., 2009). Doing so involves designing research and approaching fieldwork creatively. Writing interesting and well-composed stories may unsettle readers' established expectations. Still, such stories may present more than a consistent report that languishes in a file; it is apparent that "to make a difference, we must be read" (Jonsen, Fendt & Point, 2018, p. 56). Jonsen et al. (2018, pp. 57–58) summarize our proposal's central idea regarding creativity and impact:

> … research can – and must – be creative. If we as scholars want to take on the big questions, if we want to contribute, however modestly, toward addressing the challenging societal, cultural, economic, and technological impacts of an accelerated digital world and address some of the daunting dysfunctions and asymmetries at hand, we might need to think differently about the world, perhaps radically differently. When studying novel phenomena, we often have neither much data nor theory to test. We are thus doubly in the unknown and must imagine *new ways of researching new ways of managing and organizing* (italics in original).

Recent approaches to research allow inclusion not only of experiences in the field but also a reflexive relation to ethical research practice (see Warren, 2008). Doing so is not just valid but especially relevant when novel and creative methods, such as "narratives, photographs, organizational artefacts or even nonverbal interactions" (Bansal and Corley, 2011, p. 235) are used. For instance, writers, readers and research subjects all participate and judge the results of research (Américo & Clegg, forthcoming; Strathern, 1987; Warren, 2008). Using photography (see Warren, 2008) can communicate how it feels to work in different situations; as the adage has it, 'every picture tells a story'. Moreover, enacting qualitative research through other than purely textual representation allows the researcher to challenge mainstream theories and redirect conversations (Bansal et al., 2018).

Fiction and other styles of writing

According to Phillips (1995), 'fact' and 'fiction' may be regarded as a restricted dichotomy. Fiction does not objectify research phenomena but allows the discussion of the humour, anger, aesthetics, fears, dreams and schemes defining people's situations. As Donnelly, Gabriel and Özkazanç-Pan (2013) argue, fictional and semi-fictional narrative works well in dealing with emotions and other aesthetic themes, themes that may be difficult to order intellectually. The present book is based on the understanding that both intellectual and aesthetic knowledge work together (Elm & Taylor, 2010; Taylor, 2000). Real-world issues are addressed by merging scenic (aesthetic) and narrative (categorical) methods to trigger in readers new ways of thinking about enacting qualitative research. The idea of narrative semi-fiction, as a style of creative writing, is introduced below as a pragmatic, reflexive and ethical practice, one that considers issues of responsibility concerning fictional writing (Rhodes & Brown, 2005).

Phillips (1995) created narrative fiction as a teaching tool, a way of showing data and a method. According to Whiteman (2004, p. 263), Phillips (1995) "encouraged us to use novels, stories, plays, songs, poems, and films as legitimate objects for study and as vehicles to convey valuable organizational information that can enrich our field". These elements increase the chance of a report being accepted and read because when events and 'facts' are narrated through dramatic stories, they can arouse the imagination and emotions of readers (Green & Brock, 2000), creating surprise by disrupting expectations of an audience.

A turn to aesthetics is registered in the endorsement of narrative semi-fiction (see Taylor, 2000), highlighting the potential of 'fiction' for 'aesthetic' theorizing. Whether accomplished by aesthetic, analytic or some other framing of sense data, different narrative practices produce different forms of representation (see Warren, 2008). Rhodes and Brown (2005, p. 485) suggest that 'fiction' may be employed to consider "responsibility and ethics" as they relate to "research writing". These investigations favour an academic practice conceived as a representation of representations (Rabinow, 1986). By this is meant rendering the representations of everyday life in another form of representation. The form of the representations will be framed by rules other than those of hypothetico-deductive convention in which statistical analysis is used for disconfirming propositions.

Literary representation is a strategy with which to trigger the curiosity of readers. Curiosity can be "activated by the pleasure of learning" (Chang & Shih, 2019, p. 3), especially when the journey of learning something new is full of engrossing and persuasive stories. Narrative semi-fiction has the potential to engage the reader by combining 'fact' and 'fiction'. It adds both 'emotions' and 'ambiguities' to textual interpretation as a way of producing a method for qualitative inquiry (see Richardson, 1994; Whiteman, 2004) and a method of reality construction (Rhodes & Brown, 2005). Narrative creates gaps in knowing the possible destinations of the story. In enacting research, the curiosity that these ambiguities arouse generate new information as a means of filling the knowledge gap (Chang & Shih, 2019). The subject of research is engaged in producing the qualitative report just as much as are the readers of the stories finally told but never finally interpreted.

The character and practice of writing (narrative fiction and other styles of creative writing)

Rhodes and Brown (2005) argue that researchers must avoid narrating, representing and performing a single reality. Instead, the authors suggest that researchers need to understand the practical value of writing, which is "both a method of inquiry (Richardson, 1994, p. 483), and a method of reality construction" (Berger and Luckmann, 1966). To wit, both reflexivity and pragmatism "are important and established responses to an acknowledgement of the fictionality of research writing" (Rhodes & Brown, 2005, p. 478). Nevertheless, Rhodes and Brown (2005, p. 478) affirm that "reflexivity and pragmatism" only "partially address this question by suggesting a process of accounting for the researcher in the research text" as well as by "acknowledging the provisional and situated use value of research outcomes rather than regard them as timeless and context-free truths". Thus, for Rhodes and Brown (2005) and Rhodes (2000b), writers need to account for their textual positions in writing, positioning themselves reflexively when writing about research. For Rhodes (2001), research writing represents and narrates stories, which are different from truth claims (cf. Chia, 1996). Accordingly, their language cannot represent reality (Czarniawska, 1997), with different writings creating distinct interpretations (Rhodes, 2000a).

Rhodes and Brown (2005, p. 479) establish narrative fiction as a pragmatic, reflexive and ethical – "rather than a descriptive" – practice. However, Ng and Cock (2002) argue that reflexivity produces a relationship between writer and subject. For the authors, the reader should also be part of the text so that the naive idea that we build 'true' texts becomes impossible, such that the relationship built between subject and reader becomes less paradoxical. Styles of creative writing have the potential to engage the writer in an ethical relation with others, producing scientific texts as a joint production, allowing the reader to choose between the positions/contexts of subjects while generating new relations for readers between authors and subjects (Américo & Clegg, forthcoming; Ng & Cock, 2002; Rhodes & Brown, 2005; Strathern, 1987).

Whiteman (2004) argues that an investigation that uses narrative semi-fiction must be plausible and critical. Achieving plausibility and adopting a critical attitude can be paradoxical. Plausibility entails preserving some of the ethos of the stories involved, which can founder on the inconsistency of highly charged emotions and ambiguities. A critical attitude means adopting a practical scepticism to the accounts that subjects provide of their situations, a scepticism that can be informed by meta-narratives derived from theory. Scholars often take subjects' accounts for granted. Reports are read, mission statements accepted, strategies explained without necessarily delving deeply into the fictional work that these accounts represent. Similarly, when subjects' texts, spoken, written or otherwise communicated, are used in research, the conditions of their possibility as accounts needs to be interrogated. What are the grounds of the possibility of the texts? What assumptions and rationalities sustain them? An imaginative attitude to narrative is necessary (cf. Berends & Deken, 2021; Jarzabkowski et al., 2021), one that will always depend on readers' sensemaking and reflexive theorizing guiding interpretation.

While some authors collapse the artificial boundaries between what Czarniawska (2008) calls 'fictional and factional narrative', alternative forms of reporting investigations that mix fiction and fact in the form of narrative fiction are needed, suggests Whiteman (2004). Accordingly, the present textbook engages different genres to 'write' about 'writing qualitative research' differently (see Rhodes, 2015; 2019; Sinclair, 2013). Doing so contests the idea that 'one text has the same claim on our attention as any other' because it is various readers' relationships with the text that affirms/denies/extends the ideas inscribed therein (Strathern, 1987, p. 268).

Reading is a practice, an action. "Reading is no longer to be regarded as a passive registering of the once correct possibility of a text but may be more appropriately seen as an activity" (Clegg, 1975, p. 14). Narrative steers and directs attention to events occurring in the stories recounted (Green & Brock, 2000). The power of a text comes from its ability to persuade others to see the significance of that which is recounted (Rabinow, 1986). The text serves as "an impetus for dialogue – renewed each time one turns to it – between the reader and the author ..." (Clegg, 1975, p. 13). Without a reader, a text is just inscriptions on a page or screen. The naive idea that we report 'truth' is impossible (Ng & Cock, 2002) because any text is inseparable from its reading in a context by a reader. Beyond the relationship that reflexivity produces between writer and subject, the reader also constitutes the text. Any social science empirical research text that uses interpretive understanding of what people do and say is a dialogue based on those dialogues the author(s) have already conducted with their theories in use and with those 'lay theories' of the subjects' sensemaking.

Different narratives and forms of expression are designed and constructed to engage different genres and modes of writing connecting the writer, reader and subject (Américo & Clegg, forthcoming; Ng & Cock, 2002; Rhodes, 2015; Strathern, 1987). While much conventional social science writing may connect its writer and an imagined reader, little of it usually relates to the subjects from whom the data was appropriated in the first place. The research subjects are often an 'absent presence' in the text.

Ethics in qualitative research

That the presence of the author in the text imbues all writing with a degree of fiction, is being increasingly recognized (Rhodes & Brown, 2005). For Rhodes and Brown (2005), such recognition is only possible once writers assume greater reflexivity in the text and understand the practical value and divergent consequences that different readings/ writings can produce. Fictional writing assumes an ethical practice (Rhodes & Brown, 2005) since stories have a great power to persuade people and change beliefs.

According to Green and Brock (2000), stories 'transport' readers from the real to the narrative world, with the 'journey' changing their understanding. Therefore, ethical issues must be considered when researchers use stories to report their data and fieldwork experiences, as the narrative created can alter the readers' view of the nature of the phenomena reported in qualitative research. Narrative fiction allows a discussion of the ethical practices adopted in relation to the writer, researcher and subject.

Ethical reflexivity is a community-level concern, in which writers, readers, reviewers, interlocutors, publication outlets and research practices produce both the scientific text and the research subject, that one calls for alternative modes of representing the research subject (Hardy, Phillips & Clegg., 2001). Thus, qualitative research texts are a shared production in which there are "many voices, multiple texts, plural authorship" (e.g. Rabinow 1983; Clifford 1980; 1982). Writing ethnographically denies the illusion of "transparent description" (Webster, 1982: III) because such writing necessarily involves authorship. Nonetheless, the 'negotiated reality' of the text is the exclusive preserve of neither reader nor writer (Crapanzano, 1980; Strathern, 1987, p. 264); the sensemaking is a mutual obligation.

In enacting multiplicity, a single order (writers representing reality) turns into orders embedded both in materiality and language (of writers, readers and subjects' logics, frames, styles and justifications performing and representing complex juxtaposed, overlapped, partially connected and conflicted realities that somehow 'hold together'). Through narrative fiction, the reflexivity of "the production of knowing and known, for when subjects and objects are made together" means that "there is no external resting place for those engaged in knowing and writing" (Mol & Law, 2002, p. 20). Thus, narrative fiction can be used as a path to account for both cognitive and emotional experiences of fieldwork (Whiteman et al., 2009), making it possible to address critical, complex, multiple and ambiguous issues in enacting qualitative research (Mohrman, 2010).

All writing in a narrative form is an ethical practice (Rhodes & Brown, 2005) because "readers may experience strong emotions and motivations" (Green & Brock, 2000, p. 702), even while reading fiction. Since a reader's relationship with a text leads to the affirmation or denial of its ideas, Strathern's *Writing Culture* (1987) claims that only if the new fictions produced by qualitative researchers are persuasive can these texts suggest new relationships between writers, readers and subjects (cf. Strathern, 1987).

All research has ethical responsibilities. When designing and conducting an investigation in situ and online, it is necessary to respect ethical theories, ethical codes and professional societies' ethical guidelines for organizing (Salmons, 2016). In each chapter, when relevant, we highlight that qualitative research needs to obtain informed consent from research subjects to use their speeches and images as well as securing formal letters from one's university and the researched contexts authorizing the research. Attention should be paid to formal codes of ethics and ethical university guidelines, as well as those of professional societies and specific contexts. The reader also has an ethical responsibility: the "possibilities of reading" (Heath, 1972, p. 33) mean that their self is never absent from the text.

The book and its chapters

In this book we discuss research practice in terms of four non-linear phases, namely: (1) accessing and departing fieldwork, (2) writing the literature review, (3) collecting and analysing data and (4) enacting qualitative research through the inscriptions that we finally settle on in the processes of creative writing. The four phases are thought of as ideal types, that is, as an instrument to understand the multiple and complex realities of enacting qualitative research, entangling academic and artistic knowledge. Although we discuss them in sequence, in practice we should expect to find the phases interwoven and entangled. A new datum may suggest a new line of research or interpretation; in turn, a new and different review of the literature may be entailed. Sequencing the phases as if they were sequential is, on our part, merely a convention to produce a clear argument. The phasing is not prescriptive but analytical.

The four chapters can be assumed as four ideal type representations of phases that every researcher must undergo in enacting fieldwork but not necessarily linearly in sequence. Instead, the phases can be thought of as moments in the practice of enacting qualitative research, as common challenges that researchers assume when enacting (1) access, (2) literature review, (3) data collection/analysis and (4) writing up of qualitative research. The practice of enacting qualitative research involves numerous other phases; thus, we do not claim to be complete.

These phases were selected to consider ethical, complex, embodied, emotional, ambiguous and related aspects in enacting contemporary qualitative research using creative writing. Simultaneously, the book addresses strategies in enacting qualitative research practice in situ and online. Each chapter includes (1) statements of purpose, methodology, findings, originality and value as well as keywords; (2) boxed overviews of key thinkers; (3) expected learning outcomes; (4) end-of-chapter summaries, questions and reflective issues and (5) annotated suggestions for further reading.

Each of the phases is explored in a chapter of the book using creative writing. In each chapter, different protagonists will raise specific ethical questions, emotions and ambiguities that qualitative researchers need to face while enacting qualitative research in relationship with field access to research writing, in situ and online. Four phases of enacting qualitative research are enacted. On the one hand, such phases can and may permeate any qualitative research. On the other hand, the stories were constructed so that the reader could understand that different researchers, with(in) specific cultures and natures (cf. Castro, 2014) react in particular ways to a specific situation, in (and out of) context.

Instead of exploring all the possibilities of scientific and literary research contained in studies of a qualitative nature, we organize the book's chapters around puzzling questions that specific researchers tend to face in qualitative fieldwork. For instance, in Chapter 1, written by Américo, Fantinel and Clegg, researchers in training build access online as well as in person. For the latter, they use pet dogs and wild animals (endangered turtles) to secure access. In Chapter 2, written by Américo and Clegg, a student undertakes a literature review to develop theory (cf. Post, Sarala, Gatrell & Prescott, 2020) about a field of study that he was not aware of but that ended in radically changing his academic direction. In Chapter 3, written by Tureta, Américo and Clegg, the researcher finds himself amid a series of controversies among research subjects and experiences mixed feelings during fieldwork. The collection and analysis of data needs to consider the dynamics of how controversies develop and their implications for the phenomenon under investigation. The ambiguity and emotions that emerged in the fieldwork are presented from a story framed as a screenplay. In Chapter 4, Américo, Carniel and Clegg theorize aesthetically about inclusion, disability studies and management from the story of an idealistic teacher who approaches this social universe throughout his work experience. In the concluding chapter, Tureta, Américo and Clegg reconcile the four ideal type steps/characters of the book.

Notes

1 https://universityofleeds.zoom.us/rec/share/khhGwx8pZ_4PArvuLmLog7iU
SVGGuIxP0qo-osB36NpfckmxFSmBq1oFXoTeJBda.i7DTcdh50BZ9fy1r
2 https://scholar.google.com.br/scholar?q=allintitle%3A+%22qualitative+
research%22&hl=pt-PT&as_sdt=1%2C5&as_vis=1&as_ylo=1500&as_
yhi=1950
3 https://scholar.google.com.br/scholar?q=allintitle%3A+%22qualitative+
research%22&hl=pt-PT&as_sdt=1%2C5&as_vis=1&as_ylo=1951&as_
yhi=2010
4 https://scholar.google.com.br/scholar?q=allintitle%3A+%22qualitative+
research%22&hl=pt-PT&as_sdt=1%2C5&as_vis=1&as_ylo=2011&as_
yhi=2021

References

Aguinis, H., Pierce, C., Bosco, F. & Muslin, I. (2009). First decade of organizational research methods: Trends in design, measurement and data-analysis topics. *Organizational Research Methods*, 12, 69–112.

Alvesson, M. & Sandberg, J. (2013). *Constructing research questions: Doing interesting research*. London: Sage.

Amabile, T. M. & Pratt, M. G. (2016). The dynamic componential model of creativity and innovation in organizations: Making progress, making meaning. *Research in Organizational Behavior*, 36, 157–183.

Américo, B. L. & Clegg, S. R. (forthcoming). Disjunctions in the context of management learning: an exemplary case of narrative fiction. *Management Learning*.

Anderson, M. H. (2006). How can we know what we think until we see what we said?: A citation and citation context analysis of Karl Weick's *The Social Psychology of Organizing*. *Organization Studies*, 27(11), 1675–1692.

Anderson, M. H. & Lemken, R. K. (2019). An empirical assessment of the influence of March and Simon's *Organizations*: The realized contribution and unfulfilled promise of a masterpiece. *Journal of Management Studies*, 56(8), 1537–1569.

Bansal, P. & Corley, K. (2011). The coming of age for qualitative research: embracing the diversity of qualitative methods. *Academy of Management Journal*, 54(2), 233–237.

Bansal, P., Smith, W. K. & Vaara, E. (2018). New ways of seeing through qualitative research. *Academy of Management Journal*, 61(4), 1189–1195.

Berends, H. & Deken, F. (2021). Composing qualitative process research. *Strategic Organization*, 19(1), 134–146.

Berger, P. L., & Luckman, T. (1966). *The social construction of reality*. New York: Doubleday.

Blumer, H. (1979). *Critiques of research in the social sciences: an appraisal of Thomas and Znaniecki's* The Polish Peasant in Europe and America (Vol. 44). New York: Transaction Publishers.

Boyle, M. & Parry, K. (2007). Telling the whole story: The case for organizational autoethnography. *Culture and Organization*, 13(3), 185–190.

Bruce, T. (2019). The case for faction as a potent method for integrating fact and fiction in research. In Farquhar, S. & Fitzpatrick, E. (Eds). *Innovations in narrative and metaphor: Methodologies and practices* (pp. 57–72). Cham: Springer.

Buchanan, D. A. & Bryman, A. (2007). Contextualizing methods choice in organizational research. *Organizational Research Methods*, 10(3), 483–501.

Carlsen, A. & Dutton, J. E. (2011). *Research alive: exploring generative moments in doing qualitative research*. Copenhagen: Business School Press.

Cassell, C.; Cunliffe, A. L. & Grandy, G. (2017). *The SAGE handbook of qualitative business and management research methods*. London: Sage.

Cassell, C., Radcliffe, L. & Malik, F. (2020). Participant reflexivity in organizational research design. *Organizational Research Methods*, 23(4), 750–773.

Castro, E. V. (2014). *Cannibal metaphysics*. Minneapolis, IN: University of Minnesota Press.

Caulley, D. N. (2008). Making qualitative research reports less boring: The techniques of writing creative nonfiction. *Qualitative Inquiry*, 14(3), 424–449.

Chang, Y-Y. & Shih, H-Y. (2019). Work curiosity: A new lens for understanding employee creativity. *Human Resource Management Review*, 29(4), 1–14.

Chia, R. (1996). *Organizational analysis as deconstructive practice*. Berlin: de Gruyter.

Clegg, S. R. (1975) *Power, rule and domination: A critical and empirical understanding of power in sociological theory and organizational life*. London and Boston, MA: Routledge and Kegan Paul.

Clegg, S. R., Cunha, M. P.e., and Berti, M. (2022) Research movements and theorizing dynamics in management and organization studies. *Academy of Management Review*, 47(3), 382–401.

Clegg, S. R., Flyvbjerg, B. & Haugaard, M. (2014). Reflections on phronetic social science: a dialogue between Stewart Clegg, Bent Flyvbjerg and Mark Haugaard. *Journal of Political Power*, 7(2), 275–306.

Clegg, S. R. & Hardy, C. (2006) Representation and reflexivity. In Clegg, S. R., Hardy, C., Nord, W., and Lawrence, T. (Eds), *Handbook of organization studies* (pp. 423–444). London: Sage.

Clifford, J. (1980). Fieldwork, reciprocity, and the making of ethnographic texts: The example of Maurice Leenhardt. *Man*, 15(5), 8–32.

Clifford, J. (1982). *Person and myth: Maurice Leenhardt in the Melanesian world*. Berkeley: University of California Press.

Crapanzano, V. (1980). *Tuhami: Portrait of a Moroccan*. Chicago, IL: University of Chicago Press.

Corley, K., Bansal, P. & Yu, H. (2021). An editorial perspective on judging the quality of inductive research when the methodological straightjacket is loosened. *Strategic Organization*, 19(1), 161–175.

Cornelissen, J. (2017). Editor's comments: Developing propositions, a process model, or a typology? Addressing the challenges of writing theory without a boilerplate. *Academy of Management Review*, 42(1), 1–9.

Cornelissen, J. (2019). Imagining futures for organization studies: The role of theory and of having productive conversations towards theory change. *Organization Studies*, 40(1), 55–58.

Cornelissen, J., Höllerer, M. A. & Seidl, D. (2021). What theory is and can be: Forms of theorizing in organizational scholarship. *Organization Theory*, 2(3), 1–19.

Czarniawska, B. (1997) *Narrating the organization: Dramas of institutional identity*. Chicago, IL: University of Chicago Press.

Czarniawska, B. (2006). Doing gender unto the other: Fiction as a mode of studying gender discrimination in organizations. *Gender, Work and Organization*, 13(3), 234–252.

Czarniawska, B. (2008). Femmes fatales in finance, or women and the city. *Organization*, 15(2), 165–186.

Denzin, N. K. (2014). Writing and/as analysis or performing the world. In U. Flick (Ed.), *The SAGE handbook of qualitative data analysis* (pp. 569–584). London: Sage.

Donnelly, P. F., Gabriel, Y. & Özkazanç-Pan, B. (2013). Untold stories of the field and beyond: narrating the chaos. *Qualitative Research in Organizations and Management*, 8, 4–15.

Easterby-Smith, M., Golden-Biddle, K., & Locke, K. (2008). Working with pluralism: Determining quality in qualitative research. *Organizational Research Methods*, 11(3), 419–429.

Eisenhardt, K. M., Graebner, M. E. & Sonenshein S. (2016). Grand challenges and inductive methods: Rigor without rigor mortis. *Academy of Management Journal*, 59(4), 1113–1123.

Elm, D. R. & Taylor, S. S. (2010). Representing wholeness: Learning via theatrical productions. *Journal of Management Inquiry*, 19(2), 127–136.

Flyvbjerg, B. (2001). *Making social science matter: Why social inquiry fails and how it can succeed again*. Cambridge: Cambridge University Press.

Frost, P. J. & Stablein, R. E. (Eds). (1992). *Doing exemplary research*. London: Sage.

Gehman, J., Glaser, V. L., Eisenhardt, K. M., Gioia, D., Langley, A. & Corley, K. G. (2018). Finding theory–method fit: A comparison of three qualitative approaches to theory building. *Journal of Management Inquiry*, 27(3), 284–300.

Gioia, D. A., Corley, K. G. & Hamilton, A. L. (2013). Seeking qualitative rigor in inductive research: Notes on the Gioia methodology. *Organizational Research Methods*, 16(1), 15–31.

Glaser, B. G. & Strauss, A. L. (1967). *The discovery of grounded theory: Strategies for qualitative research*. Chicago, IL: Aldine.

Goffman, E. (1955). On face-work: An analysis of ritual elements in social interaction. *Psychiatry*, 18(3), 213–231.

Granek, L. & Nakash, O. (2016). The impact of qualitative research on the 'real world' knowledge translation as education, policy, clinical training, and clinical practice. *Journal of Humanistic Psychology*, 56(4), 414–435.

Green, M. C. & Brock, T. C. (2000). The role of transportation in the persuasiveness of public narratives. *Journal of Personality and Social Psychology*, 79(5), 701–721.

Grodal, S., Anteby, M. & Holm, A. L. (2020). Achieving rigor in qualitative analysis: The role of active categorization in theory building. *Academy of Management Review*, 46(3), 591–612.

Guba, E. G. & Lincoln, Y. S. (1985). *Naturalistic inquiry*. Beverly Hills, CA: Sage.

Hacking, I. (1992). The self-vindication of the laboratory sciences. In Pickering, A. (Ed.). *Science as practice and culture* (pp. 29–64). Chicago, IL: University of Chicago Press.

Hacking, I. (1994). Styles of scientific thinking or reasoning: A new analytical tool for historians and philosophers of the sciences. In Gavroglu, K., Christianidis, J. & Nicolaidis, E. (Eds), *Trends in the historiography of science* (pp. 31–48). Berlin: Springer.

Hardy, C. & Clegg, S. R. (1997) Relativity without relativism: Reflexivity in post-paradigm organization studies, S1–S4, *British Journal of Management*, 8 (Special Issue).

Hardy, C., Phillips, N. & Clegg, S. R. (2001) Reflexivity in organization and management theory: A study of the production of the research "subject"', *Human Relations*, 54(5), 531–560.

Harold, J. (2003). Flexing the imagination. *The Journal of Aesthetics and Art Criticism*, 61(3), 247–257.

Heath, S. (1972) *The Nouveau Roman: A study in the practice of writing*. London: Elek.

Heikkurinen, P., Clegg, S., Pinnington, A. H., Nicolopoulou, K. & Alcaraz, J. M. (2021). Managing the Anthropocene: Relational agency and power to respect planetary boundaries. *Organization & Environment*, 34(2), 267–286.

Hibbert, P., Sillince, J., Diefenbach, T. & Cunliffe, A. L. (2014). Relationally reflexive practice: A generative approach to theory development in qualitative research. *Organizational Research Methods*, 17(3), 278–298.

Humphries, M. T. & Dyer, S. (2005). Introducing critical theory to the management classroom: An exercise building on Jermier's "Life of Mike". *Journal of Management Education*, 29(1), 169–195.

Jarzabkowski, P., Langley, A. & Nigam, A. (2021). Navigating the tensions of quality in qualitative research. *Strategic Organization*, 19(1), 70–80.

Jermier, J. M. (1985). 'When the sleeper wakes': A short story extending themes in radical organization theory. *Journal of Management*, 11(2), 67–80.

Jonsen, K., Fendt, J. & Point, S. (2018). Convincing qualitative research: What constitutes persuasive writing? *Organizational Research Methods*, 21(1), 30–67.

Kashdan, T. B., Stiksma, M. C., Disabato, D. D., McKnight, P. E., Bekier, J., Kaji, J. & Lazarus, R. (2018). The five-dimensional curiosity scale: Capturing the bandwidth of curiosity and identifying four unique subgroups of curious people. *Journal of Research in Personality*, 73, 130–149.

Koning, J. & Ooi, C. S. (2013). Awkward encounters and ethnography. *Qualitative Research in Organizations and Management*, 8(1), 16–32.

Kor, Y. Y., Mahoney, J. T., Siemsen, E. & Tan, D. (2016). Penrose's *The Theory of the Growth of the Firm*: An exemplar of engaged scholarship. *Production and Operations Management*, 25(10), 1727–1744.

Land, C. & Taylor, S. (2018). Access and departure. In Cassell, C., Cunliffe, A. L. & Grandy, G. (Eds), *The SAGE handbook of qualitative business and management research methods* (Vol. 4, pp. 465–479), London: Sage.

Langley, A. (1999). Strategies for theorizing from process data. *Academy of Management Review*, 24(4), 691–710.

Latour, B. (2005). *Reassembling the social: An introduction to actor-network-theory*. Oxford: Oxford University Press.

Law, J. (2004). *After method: Mess in social science research*. London: Routledge.

Law, J. (2009). Seeing like a survey. *Cultural Sociology*, 3(2), 239–256.

Lê, J. K. & Schmid, T. (2020). The practice of innovating research methods. *Organizational Research Methods*, 1–29, doi:10.1177/1094428120935498

Learmonth, M. & Humphreys, M. (2012). Autoethnography and academic identity: Glimpsing business school doppelgängers. *Organization*, 19(1), 99–117.

Lerman, M. P., Mmbaga, N. & Smith, A. (2020). Tracing ideas from Langley (1999): Exemplars, adaptations, considerations, and overlooked. *Organizational Research Methods*, 25(2), 285–307.

Locke, K., Feldman, M. & Golden-Biddle, K. (2020). Coding practices and iterativity: Beyond templates for analyzing qualitative data. *Organizational Research Methods*, 1094428120948600.

Lofland, J., Snow, D. A., Anderson, L. & Lofland, L.H. (2006), *Analyzing social settings: A guide to qualitative observation and analysis*, 4th ed., Belmont, CA: Wardsworth.

Lounsbury, M. & Carberry, E. J. (2005). From king to court jester? Weber's fall from grace in organizational theory. *Organization Studies*, 26(4), 501–525.

Majima, S. & Moore, N. (2009). Introduction: Rethinking qualitative and quantitative methods. *Cultural Sociology*, 3(2), 203–216. https://doi.org/10.1177/1749975509105531

Miles, M. B., Huberman, A. M. & Saldana, J. (2014). *Qualitative data analysis: A methods sourcebook*. London: Sage.

Mir, R. & Jain, S. (2017). *The Routledge companion to qualitative research in organization studies*. London: Routledge.

Mohrman, S. A. (2010). Emotions, values, and methodology: Contributing to the nature of the world we live in whether we intend to or not. *Journal of Management Inquiry*, 19(4), 345–347.

Mol, A. (2002). *The body multiple: Ontology in medical practice*. Durham, NC: Duke University Press.

Mol, A. & Law, J. (2002). Complexities: An introduction. In Law, J. & Mol, A. (Eds), *Complexities: Social studies of knowledge practices* (pp. 1–23). Durham, NC: Duke University Press.

Ng, W. & Cock, C. D. (2002). Battle in the boardroom: A discursive perspective. *Journal of Management Studies*, 39(1), 23–49.

Patriotta, G. & Hirsch, P. M. (2016). Mainstreaming innovation in art worlds: Cooperative links, conventions and amphibious artists. *Organization Studies*, 37(6), 867–887.

Peticca-Harris, A., deGama, N. & Elias, S. R. (2016). A dynamic process model for finding informants and gaining access in qualitative research. *Organizational Research Methods*, 19(3), 376–401.

Phillips, N. (1995). Telling organizational tales: On the role of narrative fiction in the study of organizations. *Organization Studies*, 16(4), 625–649.

Post, C., Sarala, R., Gatrell, C. & Prescott, J. E. (2020). Advancing theory with review articles. *Journal of Management Studies*, 57(2), 351–376.

Pratt, M. 2009. From the editors: The lack of a boilerplate: Tips on writing up (and rewriting) qualitative research. *Academy of Management Journal*, 52, 856–862.

Rabinow, P. (1983). "'Facts are a word of God': An essay review," in G. W. Stocking (Ed), *Observers observed* (History of Anthropology I.) (pp. 196–207) Madison: University of Wisconsin Press.

Rabinow, P. (1986). Representations are social facts: Modernity and postmodernity in anthropology. In Clifford J. & Marcus, G. E. (Eds). *Writing culture: The poetics and politics of ethnography* (pp. 234–261). Berkeley, CA: University of California Press.

Rhodes, C. (2000a) Reading and writing organizational lives, *Organization*, 7(1), 7–29.

Rhodes, C (2000b) Ghostwriting research: Positioning the researcher in the interview text. *Qualitative Inquiry*, 6(4), 511–525.

Rhodes, C. (2001) *Writing organization: (Re)presentation and control in narratives at work*. London: John Benjamins.

Rhodes, C. (2015). Writing organization/romancing fictocriticism. *Culture and Organization*, 21(4), 289–303.

Rhodes, C. (2019). Sense-ational organization theory! Practices of democratic scriptology. *Management Learning*, 50(1), 24–37.

Rhodes, C. & Brown, A. D. (2005). Writing responsibly: Narrative fiction and organization studies. *Organization*, 12(4), 467–491.

Richardson, L. (1994). Writing: A method of inquiry. In Denzin N. K. & Lincoln Y. S. (Eds), *Handbook of qualitative research* (pp. 516–529). Thousand Oaks, CA: Sage.

Rockström, J. (2010). Planetary boundaries. *New Perspectives Quarterly*. 27(1), 72–74.

Salmons, J. E. (2016). *Doing qualitative research online*. London: Sage.

Savage, P., Cornelissen, J. P. & Franck, H. (2018). Fiction and organization studies. *Organization Studies*, 39(7), 975–994.

Shalley, C. E. & Zhou, J. (2008). Organizational creativity research: A historical overview. In Zhou, J. & Shalley, C. E. (Eds). *Handbook of organizational creativity* (pp. 3–31). New York, NY: Taylor & Francis Group.

Silverman, D. (Ed.). (2020). *Qualitative research*. London: Sage.

Silverman, D. (2022). *Doing qualitative research: A practical handbook*. London: Sage.

Sinclair, A. (2013). A material dean. *Leadership*, 9(3), 436–443.

Stanley, L. (2010). To the letter: Thomas and Znaniecki's *The Polish Peasant* and writing a life, sociologically. *Life Writing*, 7(2), 139–151.

Stengers, I. (2015). *In catastrophic times: Resisting the coming barbarism*. London: Open Humanities Press.

Strathern, M. (1987). Out of context. *Current Anthropology*, 28(3), 251–281.

Strati, A. (2009). 'Do you do beautiful things?'. Aesthetics and art in qualitative methods of organization studies. In D. Buchanan and A. Bryman (Eds). *The Sage handbook of organizational research methods* (pp. 230–245). London: Sage.

Taylor, S. S. (2000). Aesthetic knowledge in academia: Capitalist pigs at the academy of management. *Journal of Management Inquiry*, 9(3), 304–328.

Tett, G. (2021) The Fed needs a psychological toolkit, *Financial Times*, 19 June, 2021, www.ft.com/content/dc30da32–49c4–4d21–814e-084a1be5ce7a, accessed 18.06.21

Thomas, W. I. & Znaniecki, F. (1919). *The Polish peasant in Europe and America: Monograph of an immigrant group*. Chicago, IL: University of Chicago Press.

van Marrewijk, A., Veenswijk, M. & Clegg, S. R. (2010) Organizing reflexivity in designed change: The ethnoventist approach. *Journal of Organizational Change Management*, 23(3), 212–229.

Vickers, M. H. (2011). Taking a compassionate turn for workers with multiple sclerosis (MS): Towards the facilitation of management learning. *Management Learning*, 42(1), 49–65.

Vickers, M. H. (2013). Three stories – and a writer's tale: A creative writing case study of workplace bullying. *Organization Management Journal*, 10(2), 139–147.

Vickers, M. H. (2015). Stories, disability, and 'dirty' workers: Creative writing to go beyond too few words. *Journal of Management Inquiry*, 24(1), 82–89.

Warren, C. A. B. & Karner, T. (2004). *Discovering qualitative methods: Field research, interviews and analysis*. Oxford: Oxford University Press.

Warren, S. (2008). Empirical challenges in organizational aesthetics research: Towards a sensual methodology. *Organization Studies*, 29(4), 559–580.

Watson, T. J. (2000). Ethnographic fiction science: Making sense of managerial work and organizational research processes with Caroline and Terry. *Organization*, 7, 489–510.

Webster, S. (1982). Dialogue and fiction in ethnography. *Dialectical Anthropology*, 7, 91–114.

Weick, K. E. (1969) *The social psychology of organizing*. Upper Saddle River, NJ: Addison-Wesley.

Weick, K. E. (1995). *Sensemaking in organizations*. Thousand Oaks, CA: Sage.

Weick, K. E. (1999). That's moving: Theories that matter. *Journal of Management Inquiry*, 8, 134–142.

Weick, K. E. (2002). Essai: Real-time reflexivity: Prods to reflection. *Organization Studies*, 23(6), 893–898.

Weick, K. E. (2005). The pragmatics of 'really mattering' on policy issues: William Ouchi as exemplar. *Academy of Management Journal*, 48(6), 986–988.

Whiteman, G. (2004). Why are we talking inside? Reflecting on traditional ecological knowledge (TEK) and management research. *Journal of Management Inquiry*, 13(3), 261–277.

Whiteman, G. (2010). 'First you have to get outside': Reflecting on the ecological location of qualitative research. *Organization & Environment*, 23(2), 119–131. https://doi.org/10.1177/1086026610368369.7

Whiteman, G., Müller, T., & Johnson, J. M. (2009). Strong emotions at work. *Qualitative Research in Organizations and Management*, 4(1), 46–61.

Whiteman, G. & Phillips, N. (2008). The role of narrative fiction and semi-fiction in organization studies. In Barry, D. & Hansen, H. (Eds). *New approaches in management and organization* (pp. 288–299). Los Angeles, CA: Sage.

Whiteman, G., Walker, B. & Perego, P. (2013). Planetary boundaries: Ecological foundations for corporate sustainability. *Journal of Management Studies*, 50(2), 307–336.

1 Accessing fieldwork

Bruno Luiz Américo, Letícia Dias Fantinel and Stewart Clegg

Keywords: Qualitative research; fieldwork access; access as data; narrative semi-fiction.

Expected learning outcomes

At the end of the chapter, readers – researchers, students, early career or otherwise – will be able to:

- Recognize the necessity of negotiating access to fieldwork.
- Ensure informed consent is obtained from research subjects.
- Know the relevance of formal codes of conduct of the university and the organization(s) researched.
- Appreciate the importance of registering observations and inscribing or recording field notes.
- Understand the significance of acting reciprocally with research subjects.
- Be sensitive about informal codes of fieldwork access.
- Distinguish ethical debates around social research, ethics codes and professional societies' ethical guidelines for organizing.
- Design and conduct an ethical qualitative investigation that is not delimited in its political potential, with contributions to academic debate and for other interested publics.

Introduction

We present a narrative semi-fiction, which "may work well as a qualitative method for exploring empirical reality and pulling together

DOI: 10.4324/9781003198161-2

fragments from fieldwork" (Whiteman & Phillips, 2008, p. 296), detailing how early career researchers negotiated access to fieldwork and moved from access challenges to research insights informing teaching and research.

As scholars, we have engaged with writers writing about creative writing (cf. Caulley, 2008; Ketelle, 2004; Whiteman, 2004; Whiteman & Phillips, 2008; Vickers, 2010, 2011) as an aspect of research. Their interpretations of how to use data have promoted debates about writing as a means of informing change (Beavan et al., 2021) as well as scientific representation in theoretical work. We use narrative semi-fiction (Whiteman & Phillips, 2008) as a tool to create a dynamic story that will, we trust, connect with our readers. We do so on the understanding that all writing, as a representation of something other than itself, is a fiction (Strathern, 1987) constructed by virtue of the authority of its narrative. Such authority is inescapably selective in emphasizing some aspects rather than others of whatever matters to which it attends (Bruce, 2019).

Overcoming the crises of representation

Science and technology studies, actor-network theory and pragmatic philosophers have all contributed to overcoming the crisis of representation, that is, the subject/object distinction that guides the production of knowledge as a neutral and objective human activity rather than a construction. Additionally, when it comes to unsettling scientific representation, there are important lessons to be learned from feminist studies. For instance, Strathern (1987) taught us that the paradoxical effect of feminist writings was to show that scientific texts are not necessarily accurate or true but plural realities that are judged (affirmed, denied, extended) by readers, writers and subjects (cf. Rabinow, 1986; Strathern, 1987).

Aligned with feminist studies, instead of describing fieldwork stories through constructs and the relationship between constructs, we use narrative semi-fiction. Writing differently, using this approach, has an essential role in social research (Huopalainen, 2020); it allows investigators to establish an ethical and reflexive relationship with heterogeneous interlocutors, events and multiple realities (Rhodes and Brown, 2005) and not delimit their research's political potential (Contu, 2020; Collins, 2012; Taylor, 2015; Land et al., 2018).

Researchers must account for themselves, their commitments, the events studied reflexively, as well as heterogeneous research interlocutors, including multiple embodied natures (e.g., as, we shall discuss, overworked and poorly trained attendants, professional colleagues, companion species and endangered turtles) and socio-material realities (e.g., as we shall discuss, protocols, organizational strategies, inscriptions and meaningful spaces) in gaining and maintaining access to fieldwork. In doing so, we produce a disciplined reflexivity (Weick, 2002) about how to negotiate access to the field of study *with* heterogeneous subjects, multiple natures and complex events.

We purposely confuse our identity (we/us) with the depicted selves (the characters of the chapter) in what follows, as we have intentionally blurred the boundaries between what could be called fact and fiction; our narrative is done but not fully fashioned, formed or finished (Haraway, 2003). The characters represented are early career researchers enrolled for an Advanced Qualitative Research course, in which the instructor required them to develop fieldwork skills by engaging with organizational members in their specific substantive fields of interest. The researchers were encouraged to write field notes to elaborate their experiences as data.

Next, we want you, the reader, to have freedom in interpreting the story and so a narrative semi-fiction is introduced. The text deals with the political and socio-material fact that subjects, as well as authorizing or disallowing access to fieldwork, continuously experience and judge the research (and the researcher), events, their selves and other relationships, their context and companions, through their intuiting of what a research purpose is and who and what is the researcher (cf. Strathern, 1987).

A day at the postgraduate course

The university's postgraduate course offered, in the first half of 2016, the subject 'Advanced Qualitative Research'.

During the first class, Professor Angela introduced herself and encouraged students to introduce themselves. Peter, one of the four students, presented himself as a researcher interested in socio-materiality and education management: "I am concerned with the reorganization of the public school in Vila Regência, in the face of the greatest environmental crime produced by mining activities in our country." He was followed by Erika, who was developing her research at the company responsible for the mining activities; she questioned the reference made to the word 'crime', indicating that the company had not yet been tried for the environmental 'tragedy'. She also highlighted the role of Vale S/ A for the State of Espírito Santo and its commitment to local people, including the communities affected by the 'catastrophe'. Peter laughed. Erika did not like it and insisted on disagreeing but was interrupted by William, colonel of the state's military police, studying the subject as a part of his management degree, who tried to anticipate what Vale's first action to reverse the negative consequences of the dam rupture would be: "changing their logo". Everyone laughed except for Erika. William took the opportunity to introduce himself and said: "I am going to study the recent structural and process modifications of the Call Centre for Social Defence (CCSD)." Finally, Gene presented herself: "I am an animal rights activist, and I am interested in organized multispecies relations in the city of Vitória."

Angela took a moment to observe the blindingly bright and warm sunlight streaming down on the students who, in the unsustainable comfort of the air conditioning, were enjoying the light playing on the garden outside the building. Then she commented on the exciting mix of people's interests in the classroom. Next, Angela read the subject outline with the class. The initial introduction was followed by a presentation of the assessment methodology of the subject, consisting of a response to the day's challenge (40 per cent of the subject grade consisting of varied activities on the topic discussed in each class); production of field notes from an observation activity in a field chosen by each student (30 per cent of the subject grade), as well as elaboration of an ethnographic exercise designed to produce inferences from empirical data (30 per cent of the subject grade). Then, the professor presented the schedule of activities and the references that supported the class. Finally, after explaining the activities and answering questions, Angela dismissed the class.

The class on access/departure

The second class addressed negotiating, gaining and maintaining access to fieldwork. It started with Angela posing some challenges to the students regarding aspects of the texts scheduled for that meeting. That day, the challenge was to answer some questions based on a dilemma in which a fictional researcher needed to choose an organization in which to carry out the fieldwork. Each of the students interpreted the class texts differently. Once the challenge stage ended, the professor sought to build a dialogue with the students:

"Class, gaining and maintaining access is a topic of growing interest", she stopped, held her breath, closed her eyes, that were beginning to water, before sneezing.

Seminal texts on access instruct investigators to manage impressions, obtain formal approvals, deploy access through networking, act reciprocally with the subject, not make explicit the research design nor judge subjects' practices. Currently, access has come to be understood as a process, in political terms, in time and space. But please tell me, what else do these texts tell us?

With no immediate takers for a reply, she prompted, "Past scholarship provides evidence that although negotiating access is a long-standing topic of study, how we gain access has been changing."

William lowered his head and held a finger up as if asking for a minute. "Cunliffe and Alcaldipani (2016) is an exemplary publication for my research; it offers a historical perspective on access research and stresses that strategies for achieving successful access are increasingly problematized." Erika interjected that, "Land and Taylor (2018) argue that there are many reflective, political and fluid reports about the practice of gaining and maintaining access in organizations", she read from their text before putting it down and picking up another one, before continuing with her reasoning. "For instance, Pettica-Harris, de Gama & Elias (2016) narrated stories about their own (un)successful access; a researcher can integrate the formulation of an initial study with plans and identify, contact and interact with potential informants."

"Using Cunliffe and Alcadipani's (2016) metalanguage, one could say that Pettica-Harris et al. (2016) indicate that gaining/maintaining access entangles the researcher with the powerful practices of the investigated organizations", says William, drawing on his interests. "Both exemplary publications embrace the idea of sharing agency between researchers and organizational members." Picking up the theme, "Cunliffe and Alcadipani (2016) conceptualize three perspectives on access: instrumental, transactional and relational", said Angela, speaking while simultaneously standing up and pushing her chair back with a scrape. "I want to ask you a question: which of these access perspectives would you embrace to develop your thesis?"

"As a colonel", said William, his eyes wide and shining, "as an insider, I am embracing the relational perspective on access, for sure. It is necessary to consider the impact of the agency of the research subjects, that is, my colleagues, on the final format of the published research."

"And what about the impact of your published research on you, your colleagues, the department studied, the police force in general?" Peter said as he opened the computer, entering the password while telling himself, 'I might have sounded rude!'. "Are you not too focused on human subjects, such as researchers and gatekeepers? For Land and Taylor

(2018), for example, social media breaks down the formal boundaries of organizations."

"Why turn to social media when I can observe and interview in action? Moreover, in the call centre, I cannot interview the computer, the telephone." Laughing out loud, he posed another question, "Or can I?" "You are joking, but you should read Nyberg (2009) instead of joking." Visibly disturbed, Peter continued, saying,

> In studying a call centre, Daniel Nyberg demonstrated how the organizational configuration was violated when the computer sent, for example, a letter to a customer without direct command, leading his research to new relationships, categories and actors. Could non-human entities cut CCSD's configuration?

"The idea that access to organizations must comprise not only human relationships was pushed further by Aroles (2020)", said Gene, while drinking water calmly, as if she had not noticed that the mood was changing.

> Jeremy Aroles observed that scientists in the forest needed to renegotiate access in every group in which they stopped; kava roots, gifted to the chiefs, secured their action as intermediaries between the forest's spirit and the scientist as a donor.

"For you, who will work with a multispecies perspective, this text is exemplary." Erika measured her words before continuing: "For me, it does not make any sense!"

"But don't you want to study Vale S/A, a company facing its worst crisis ever?", Gene said while raising her eyebrow.

> This text can help you understanding if the severity and longevity of the impact of Vale's tailings mud from its burst dam on the *Rio Doce* and its fauna act as mediators and agencies in the design of the organization's strategy. And it is important to remember that dealing with non-human agency in research is not about giving human characteristics to other beings or objects. It is a kind of ontological turn that helps us to remove the human from the centre of the analysis and consider other agencies on their own terms.

"I might be wrong, but as she is an insider, in step with Taylor (2015), I bet her research will be delimited in its political potential", spoke

William, as he took some printed texts from his backpack. "From what I gather from reading these texts, Ho (2009) got her Wall Street job but failed to access the data she expected for her critical research."

"I agree with both Gene and William", said Erika, contradicting everyone's expectations, as demonstrated by other people's reactions.

> How will my peers react to the news that I, a young black woman, will presume to research such a pale stale masculine environment? The race, gender and ideology of both researchers and researched shapes the research sample, what can even be researched, as Blee (2002) tells us; I am aware that my investigation might prove to be a tremendously 'awkward encounter'[1]!

"The discussion is going well, but ...", Angela said as she pointed to her mobile phone, making everyone laugh, some desperately and others forcibly. "Unfortunately, the clock keeps ticking down and we must shortly finish the class."

Before ending the class, the professor summarized the texts they were going to be using, stating that access should no longer be conceptualized strictly as a technical problem but as a relationship involving political negotiations in which the field and the researcher engaged each other in different ways. Finally, Angela announced that there will be no classes on the next two weeks as planned: "We meet again in fifteen days, and the next class's challenge will be different; you will have to talk about how your fieldwork access negotiation went – meaning that fieldwork starts right away for you!"

Peter and Gene, who were granted a federal government scholarship, could dedicate themselves entirely to fieldwork. Erika and William, who worked full-time in the organizations where their own investigation would take place, would come to experience their respective positions differently.

Fifteen days go fast when you are waiting for something

"Welcome back, everybody! I am curious; I am looking forward, actually! Since we are all gathered already, who may do the honours?" Angela, trying to contain her excitement, directs visual contact to the students' eyes. "Great William, take it away."

> For the last five years, I have worked with Geoprocessing, Statistics and Criminal Analysis services at the State Secretariat for Public Security (SSPS). Now, I am working with strategic management,

coordinating the implementation of the Call Centre for Social Defence (CCSD).

Nervously, he walks to the door, then back to the centre of the room, bringing his hands from his hair to his eyes; a voice muffled, sounding regretful.

I assumed my new position the same day we had our first class. As a public agent, while I am used to handovers, I have to confess that it felt like there was too much on for me at this time.

"Are you okay, William? You are worrying me!" Angela breathes in, breathes out, and continues: "Was it too much working and starting the research at the same time?"

"I do not know." Now, standing in the centre of the room, William shook his shoulders indifferently.

What can I tell you about working and researching? The list of potential 'informants' is more extensive and heterogeneous than I thought. I had just imagined a short questionnaire and a few interviews from which I could report the results. The books we are reading present too much, too much complexity, when I thought it was just about talking to people, but it seems that it includes everything, from machines to protocols and attendants; if they are not aligned, they can bother us a lot!

Abruptly, William said, "I've got to leave; I am sorry!" He gathered his things with the haste of someone visibly discomforted. He opened the door and ran out, leaving it wide open. Angela got up immediately, walked to the door seemingly intent on following him running down the hall. When she saw William leaving the building, she went back to the classroom. She closed the door and stood there, staring through the glass window of the door. Peter interrupted the silence, his voice sounding loud in the stillness of the room.

"Do you think joining the new position and researching was too much for him?" He took a deep breath, straightening his back. "Did anyone talk to him before class?"

"Last week, I saw William in the news, at a glance, while I had lunch close to work. I think a news report about CCSD's failure to assist an app driver." Erika frowned, searching her memory as if she were looking for a book in an extensive library. "Gosh, I just remembered that the driver died; it was a complex case involving everything from the car's emergency connection to the outsourced security company, including the police's protocol failure that led to other actions and mistakes."

"Let us give William some space", said Angela, not sure about the best decision in this case. "Shall we stay in class until the break?"

"Ok, then I can go next." Looking at the door's window, Erika started. "My workplace is also my research field. However, while access to data occurs in action for William, my access has been restricted in its critical potential by only being allowed to do online data collection." Looking at the faces of her fellow students she noted that they looked perplexed – she was not sure what to say to explain her situation.

"You can write research with online data only, for instance", said Angela, coming to her assistance, seeing Erika's helplessness. Angela continued. "You have the job, but not the access to sensitive, classified data? ... So, are you writing about the closed professional culture of this mining company?"

"I believe I had my access denied due to my objective of understanding the process of organizational learning with the collapse of two dams in less than three years." With a determined look, Erika kept talking, without answering Angela's question.

> When talking to my colleagues and superiors about the research, I had the impression that they were trying to persuade me to 'be more comprehensive' with Vale S/A's actions after the socio-environmental tragedies that occurred; perhaps because they cannot say that the company learnt anything from one catastrophe to the next. And now I believe that my colleagues and my boss are suspicious of me because I do not believe the company's rhetoric. I am afraid I will suffer some kind of reprisal, or even lose my job, depending on what I write or publish.

Erika tried to continue, with her voice faltering. Everyone remained silent, understanding the impact of those words. Angela took the floor and talked about the risks of contradicting corporate interests with our research. These risks exist and we cannot be naive to believe that what we research, write or publish cannot cause us problems, she said. And she continued:

> This is a very delicate issue, and it is essential that we reflect on it. In general, we talk about the risks of research to informants, but we say little about the risks to the researcher. And one of the most obvious risks is losing access to the field.

Angela continued talking about the strange encounters produced in accessing fieldwork and the impossibility of being fully prepared for the beginning of the research as well as how easy it was to be shut out of a research site by an executive decision.

"As part of Vale S/A, Erika's research voice could serve noble social justice causes, such as the movement of those affected by dams." Weighing the negative side of such a critical stance, Angela declared:

> However, speaking truth to power in your case can have negative consequences, personally. Either way, just make sure you assess the meaning of your investigation, your role in public life and how to communicate your research findings to the public.

"Peter is coming next, am I right?"

> Yes, I am. Thank you. My research also intends to serve social movements of those affected by dams in general and, particularly, Vila Regência, at the mouth of the *Rio Doce*. This is where the 62 million cubic tons of mud flowed when the *Fundão* dam collapsed on November 5, 2015.

Looking up from his notes, he continued.

> I rented a house next to the school after our last class. When the research I was doing started to look at the Final Grades of Primary Education at the local school, the *Escola Estadual de Ensino Fundamental e Médio Vila Regência* (EEEFM VR), the headmistress, Maria, made herself clear: 'you can have access to all school spaces except for the classroom. Into the classroom, only if teachers invite you'.

"And?" Angela, widened her eyes and shrugged her shoulders, followed by asking, "Did you receive an invitation?"

> Teachers have not invited me yet. Nobody was willing to talk or be observed because the village is under the media spotlight due to the environmental disaster. In addition, the political disturbance we are living through in Brazil has reached the schools. Radical right-wing groups are claiming that educational professionals are captured by 'cultural Marxism'. Teachers are afraid of suffering persecution, so the atmosphere is not suitable for observations into the classroom. They are worried that I may be a spy of the government.

What to do in this case, Erika thought; she asked, "How do you intend to proceed?"

> I have two plans, actually! I intend to gain and maintain the trust of the school's professionals by assisting them in developing educational projects; the school provides education through projects that inquire into critical aspects of Vila Regência, such as the toxic mud in the Rio Doce, which projects they submit for awards for best practices in education. These prizes generate individual, collective and organizational and environmental benefits. However, the school's teachers complain that the interdisciplinary efforts needed for projects generates extra work for them. I intend to cultivate a relationship with them by supporting them with project writing in step with the awards guidelines.

Practice, however clever, may well differ from the theory, Erika thought. "It may take a while to gain the professionals' trust."

"Without a doubt, Erika!" Entering again the discussion in which the class was becoming immersed, Peter followed.

> EEEFM VR is one of the 497 schools of the Espírito Santo Education Network; while I cannot access employees' narratives, I am able to discuss the different uses of rules and regulations in education within the school. These constitute what it does, so I am looking at these to get the investigation started. I am mapping regulations that prescribe the action that constitutes work in the school. Then, I am looking at the organizational inscriptions produced, such as school reports and educational projects; these materialize education in relationship to spaces that are meaningful for the school community, such as the local rivers and riparian forests. I am talking about multiple natures, such as endangered turtles, the focus of some of the educational projects of the school, which is collaborating with other organizations, such as the Tamar Project, the environmentalists.

"What does Tamar have to do with your research", questioned Angela, gesturing for Peter to continue.

> Tamar began its activities in Vila Regência in 1980. By the 1990s, Tamar was frequently contacting the school, searching for common interests. This conservation organization is involved in environmental education and schoolchildren comprise part of its audience. The school sought to improve its education provision through

strategic partnerships, which proved successful. When accessing the Tamar Project, I got to know biologists who have been working with the school since 1990.

When Peter finished his presentation, Gene followed.

"Well, as you know, my research takes place at the Zoonosis Surveillance Centre (ZSC), linked to the municipal government." She sighed, scribbling something in the notebook on her lap.

In my case, as it is a public office, I had to deal with two dimensions of access. One of them is bureaucratic, having all the necessary formal permissions. Without these permissions, I am not even allowed to enter the downtown building as a researcher. This process took a little more time than I expected but it was only the beginning. Now, I must gain people's trust but, surprisingly for me, it is not the formal and official permissions that are making it easier to engage them.

"Oh, no?" Angela asked, leaning on the table at the front of the room. The rest of the class also listened intently and were curious as to how the access was negotiated. "So, what is making it easier for you?"

"It is not *what*, it is *who*." Gene shifted in her chair and giggled out of the corner of her mouth, showing confidence.

I had adopted my rescue dog few years ago from the municipal shelter (the shelter is a part of the ZSC), and when I showed people there her pictures on my phone, some of the employees there remembered her. I took her twice to the building and it was a big success! Lucky me, she remembered them as well, and that day was memorable for my fieldwork. Now everybody knows who I am, what my research is about, they come to talk to me and ask about my investigation, ask to participate in it, ask me to bring my dog in again… Somehow, they appear to think I am trustworthy because I care for the dog that once was the sweetheart of the shelter. So, part of the job of conquering people's confidence in the field is being made by her! I'm so excited and thankful to her that I am considering making a tattoo with my dog's face! Am I crazy or what?

She asked this question with a big smile.

Everybody laughed. Angela took the opportunity to take on the difficult but necessary activity of summarizing all those emotional, ambiguous, compassionate, judgmental, complex and multiple narratives. Based on readings as well as classroom debate and fieldwork experience, they discussed researchers and subjects, natures, materiality and beings, in terms of various assemblages, affordances, enactments and consequences. The class learned that different heterogeneous interlocutors could have an important role in our fieldwork, making them realize that they have little or no control over the participants in their fieldwork. They learnt that they should seek to enact multiple relationships to help in the ongoing negotiation of fieldwork access. Finishing the subject, they left the classroom and headed off to the canteen to grab a coffee.

Gathering sensitive encounters over coffee

William was there when they arrived at the canteen, looking partially embarrassed, partially grateful for everybody's discretion and empathy: "Thank you guys, I do not know what happened with me in there." Nobody said a word; they just gathered around William and after the first hug, they all hugged him firmly. He was apparently calm.

Before the class started, some students considered themselves mainly as practitioners, while others believed themselves to be researchers. However, now, after fieldwork, they all looked at each other with mutual respect, understanding the importance of their professions but also of acting as researchers in training; they felt a similar excitement about the possibilities of finding data in many different things and ways.

Final considerations

Our objective was to use narrative semi-fiction to guide scholars seeking to negotiate access to collect qualitative data for research. Notably, we have linked up with narrative semi-fiction to reflect on how different researchers in training move from access challenges to research insights. Our narrative demonstrates that to negotiate access to research sites, researchers must reflexively account for themselves, their commitments, the events studied as well as the heterogeneous research interlocutors, including multiple embodied natures (e.g., overworked and poorly trained attendants, professional colleagues, companion species, endangered turtles) and socio-material realities (e.g., protocols, organizational strategies, inscriptions, meaningful spaces) entangled with their investigations. The story illustrates access stumbles that can lead to research insights and socio-material data.

Questions

1   After reading the story, what are the take-aways for you from this narrative semi-fiction?
2   What has it added to your understanding about negotiating access and doing fieldwork today?
3   How does the story you have just read resonate with your experiences?
4   What have you learnt from the experience of each of the characters and how can you bring it to your research practice and experience?

Next, there are some reflective questions to plan the start of *your* qualitative research. There is also a table indicating complementary literature. Read and think!

Reflective issues

Reflexively, try to answer these important to remember questions as a few essential points before negotiating access to fieldwork:

- Do you have a field notebook? Have you research*ed online* about the organization to be studied?
- Based on your initial research, can you define what the studied organization produces and how it organizes its production historically? (Not always an easy question; think of the school – what does it produce?)
- What practices and objects are employed by the organization you will study?
- What other organizations, beings, natures and elements are related to the organization that you propose to study? How important is it to build a relationship with these heterogeneous subjects? How would you build such relationships?

Complementary readings

Table 1 offers reading suggestions related to fieldwork access.

Table 1 Complementary readings on accessing fieldwork

Related methodological themes	Comments	Reading suggestions
Field notebook	The field notebook, the definition of which is imprecise, varying with projects, demands constant research and analysis by the researcher	Cefai (2013b), Clifford (1990), Emerson, Fretz and Shaw (2001), Fine (1993), Jackson (1990)
Ethnography as a research strategy and method	Ethnography makes it possible to describe people's everyday life through immersion and prolonged observation in the field.	Atkinson, Coffey, Delamont, Lofland and Lofland (2001), Cefai (2013a), Pandeli, Sutherland and Gaggiotti (2022), Wagner (2016); Ybema, Yanow, Wels and Kamsteeg (2009)
Inscriptions	Analyses recognizing that the action does not belong to a specific body or location.	Cooper (1989), Czarniawska (2004), Derrida (1974), Latour and Woolgar (1986)
Building exemplary research	Exemplary research allows for thinking about the research practice.	Frost and Stablein (1992), Pratt (2009), Silverman (2022)

Source: Prepared by the authors.

Note

1 Koning and Ooi (2013).

References

Aroles, J. (2020). Ethnographic encounters: Towards a minor politics of field access. *Culture and Organization*, 26(1), 48–60.

Atkinson, P., Coffey, A., Delamont, S., Lofland, J. & Lofland, L. (Eds) (2001). *Handbook of ethnography*. London: Sage.

Beavan, K., Borgström, B., Helin, J. & Rhodes, C. (2021). Changing writing/ writing for change. *Gender, Work and Organization*, 28(2), 449–455.

Blee, K. M. (2002). *Inside organized racism: Women in the hate movement*. Berkeley: University of California Press.

Bruce, T. (2019). The case for faction as a potent method for integrating fact and fiction in research. In Farquhar, S. & Fitzpatrick, E. (Eds). *Innovations in* narrative and metaphor: Methodologies and practices* (pp. 57–72). Singapore, SG: Springer.

Caulley, D. N. (2008). Making qualitative research reports less boring: The techniques of writing creative nonfiction. *Qualitative Inquiry*, 14(3), 424–449.

Cefaï, D. (2013a). Qué es la etnografía? Debates contemporáneos Primera parte. Arraigamientos, operaciones y experiencias del trabajo de campo. *Persona y Sociedad*. 27(1), 101–120.

Cefaï, D. (2013b). Qué es la etnografía? Segunda parte. Inscripciones, extensiones y recepciones del trabajo de campo. *Persona y Sociedad*, 27(3), 11–32.

Clifford, J. (1990). Notes on Field(notes). In: R. Sanjek (org.), *Fieldnotes: The making of anthropology* (pp. 47–70). Ithaca, NY: Cornell University Press..

Collins, P. H. (2012). *On intellectual activism*. Philadelphia, PA: Temple University Press.

Contu, A. (2020). Answering the crisis with intellectual activism: Making a difference as business schools scholars. *Human Relations*, 73(5), 737–757.

Cooper, R. (1989). Modernism, post modernism and organizational analysis 3: The contribution of Jacques Derrida. *Organization Studies*, 10(4), 479–502.

Cunliffe, A. L. & Alcadipani, R. (2016). The politics of access in fieldwork: Immersion, backstage dramas, and deception. *Organizational Research Methods*, 19(4), 535–561.

Czarniawska, B. (2004). On time, space, and action nets. *Organization*, 11(6), 773–791.

Derrida, J. (1974). *Of grammatology* (G. C. Spivak, Trans.). Baltimore, MD: Johns Hopkins University Press.

Emerson, R. M., Fretz, R. I. & Shaw, L. L. (2001). Participant observation and fieldnotes. In Atkinson, P., Coffey, A., Delamont, S., Lofland J. and Lofland, L. (Eds), *Handbook of ethnography* (pp. 352–368). London: Sage.

Fine, G. A. (1993). Ten lies of ethnography: Moral dilemmas of field research. *Journal of Contemporary Ethnography*, 22(3), 267–294.

Frost, P. J. & Stablein, R. E. (Eds). (1992). *Doing exemplary research*. London: Sage.

Haraway, D. J. (2003). *The companion species manifesto: Dogs, people, and significant otherness*. Chicago, IL: Prickly Paradigm Press.

Ho, K. (2009). *An ethnography of Wall Street*. Durham, UK: Duke University Press.

Huopalainen, A. (2020). Writing with the bitches. *Organization*. 1–10.

Jackson, J. E. (1990). 'Deja entendu': The liminal qualities of anthropological fieldnotes. *Journal of Contemporary Ethnography*, 19(1), 8–43.

Ketelle, D. (2004). Writing truth as fiction: Administrators think about their work through a different lens. *Qualitative Report*, 9(3), 449–462.

Koning, J. & Ooi, C.-S. (2013). Awkward encounters and ethnography. *Qualitative Research in Organizations and Management: An International Journal*, 8(1), 16–32.

Land, C. & Taylor, S. (2018). Access and departure. In Cassell, C., Cunliffe, A. L. & Grandy, G. (Eds) *The SAGE handbook of qualitative business and management research methods* (Vol. 4, pp. 465–479). London: Sage.

Latour, B. & Woolgar, S. (1986). *Laboratory life: The construction of scientific facts*. Princeton, NJ: Princeton University Press.

Nyberg, D. (2009). Computers, customer service operatives and cyborgs: Intra-actions in call centres. *Organization Studies*, 30(11), 1181–1199.

Pandeli, J., Sutherland, N. & Gaggiotti, H. (2022). *Organizational ethnography: An experimental and practical guide*. New York, NY: Routledge.

Peticca-Harris, A., deGama, N. & Elias, S. R. (2016). A dynamic process model for finding informants and gaining access in qualitative research. *Organizational Research Methods*, 19(3), 376–401.

Pratt, M. G. (2009). From the editors: For the lack of a boilerplate: Tips on writing up (and reviewing) qualitative research, *Academy of Management Journal*, 52(5), 856–862.

Rabinow, P. (1986). Representations are social facts: Modernity and post-modernity in anthropology. In Clifford, J. & Marcus G. E. (Eds), *Writing culture: The poetics and politics of ethnography* (pp. 234–261). Berkeley, CA: University of California Press.

Rhodes, C. & Brown, A. D. (2005). Writing responsibly: Narrative fiction and organization studies. *Organization*, 12(4), 467–491.

Silverman, D. (2022). *Doing qualitative research: A practical handbook*. London: Sage.

Strathern, M. (1987). Out of context. *Current Anthropology*, 28(3), 251–281.

Taylor, R. (2015). Beyond anonymity: Temporality and the production of knowledge in a qualitative longitudinal study. *International Journal of Social Research Methodology*, 18(3), 281–292.

Vickers, M. H. (2010). The creation of fiction to share other truths and different viewpoints: A creative journey and an interpretive process. *Qualitative Inquiry*, 16(7), 556–565.

Vickers, M. H. (2011). Taking a compassionate turn for workers with multiple sclerosis (MS): Towards the facilitation of management learning. *Management Learning*, 42(1), 49–65.

Wagner, R. (2016). *The invention of culture*. Chicago, IL: University of Chicago Press.

Weick, K. E. (2002). Essai: Real-time reflexivity: Prods to reflection. *Organization Studies*, 23(6), 893–898.

Whiteman, G. (2004). Why are we talking inside? Reflecting on traditional ecological knowledge (TEK) and management research. *Journal of Management Inquiry*, 13(3), 261–277.

Whiteman, G. & Phillips, N. (2008). The role of narrative fiction and semi-fiction in organization studies. In Barry. D. & Hansen, H. (Eds), *New approaches in management and organization* (pp. 288–299). Los Angeles, CA: Sage.

Ybema, S., Yanow, D., Wels, H. & Kamsteeg, F. (Eds). (2009). *Organizational ethnography: Studying the complexities of everyday life*. London: Sage.

2   Reviewing the literature, developing theory?

Bruno Luiz Américo and Stewart Clegg[1]

Keywords: Organization theory; literature review; empirical method; research-based narrative fiction; post-modernism.

Expected learning outcomes

At the end of the chapter, readers will be able to:

- Understand the importance of finding exemplary publications to write a literature review to develop theory and think about their investigations and fieldwork.
- Use exemplary publications to write the literature review to develop theory.

Introduction

We present an empirical method for gaining insight from exemplary publications that allows students and investigators to write literature reviews to develop theory. The approach is one that grew out of our experience working together as professor and student. To represent this experience and tell its story, we produce a research-based narrative fiction (Vickers, 2010, 2011, 2015; Whiteman & Phillips, 2008) about how the method was created and employed to develop organization theory. It is conventional to begin research by conducting a literature review. If everything proceeds according to plan, which it rarely does, this will work out fine. More likely, you will do an initial literature review and then be guided by your research findings as you collect more data and make more observations. These can oftentimes take you in a different direction. Nonetheless, the approach that we outline is useful to adopt at any stage in the research.

DOI: 10.4324/9781003198161-3

A literature review can be defined "as a study that analyses and synthesizes an existing body of literature by identifying, challenging, and advancing the building blocks of a theory through an examination of a body (or several bodies) of prior work" (Post, Sarala, Gatrell & Prescott, 2020, p. 352). Literature reviews are important in enabling the consolidation of fragmented, interdisciplinary and scattered knowledge about a topic or research area, from one or more fields of study, topics or domains, summarizing the insights and knowledge claims that were compiled in an integrative and generative way (Baumeister & Leary, 1997; Cropanzano, 2009; Gatrell & Breslin, 2017; Kunisch, Menz, Bartunek, Cardinal & Denyer, 2018; Post et al., 2020; Snyder, 2019; Torraco, 2005; 2016; Webster & Watson, 2002). Therefore, literature reviews provide emergent platforms, conceptualizations and directions for advancing knowledge (Jones & Gatrell, 2014), facilitating the development of theory (Breslin, Gatrell & Bailey, 2020; Webster & Watson, 2002) that is grounded in the genealogy of a field that can challenge traditional paradigms and set out new theoretical routes (Breslin et al., 2020; Suddaby, Hardy & Huy, 2011; Weick, 1989).

With the growth of knowledge production in a field, studies dedicated to reviewing the literature become increasingly important (Kunisch et al., 2018; Snyder, 2019); literature reviews allow theory to develop in association with evidence, controversies and methods specifically designed to address significant matters (e.g. Kilduff, 2006; Van Maanen, Sørensen & Mitchell, 2007). However, there are a few methodological guidelines on how to produce literature reviews (Denyer & Tranfield, 2009; Kunisch et al., 2018). Conversely, "there is a need to advance our knowledge about the methodological approaches for conducting such research" (Kunisch et al., 2018, p. 520), giving "scholars a more complete set of methodological tools to address important questions" (Anderson & Lemken, 2020, p. 2).

We will describe how we have relied on Strathern (1987) to create and use an empirical method to examine how theories are used, empirically tested and denied, a method that can be used to map disjunctions in a field. Strathern (1987) showed how British Social Anthropology in the 1920s went from Frazer's dense literary description (historical and anachronic) to Malinowski's contextualized/scientific description (holist and synchronic). The new writing produced by Malinowski uses fieldwork and description to place the research subject in a social context, organizing a monograph to compare contexts and making accounts that explored the everyday mythology of the experiences encountered. Doing this was in contra-distinction to Frazer (1825), for whom there was no theoretical reason to make the exotic something ordinary, since the ordinary and extraordinary are positioned as functionally similar in a text without context, one that unites differences. For Strathern (1987), Frazer's writing, by not taking village social organization seriously, could be revisited in the face of a postmodern turn.

For Strathern, these two exemplars – Frazer and Malinowski – invite reflection on how to think about different levels of context in anthropological writing, as well as in the collection and analysis of data, the emergent contexts of production and dissemination of work and the multiple uses made of the work for later quotations. The ethnographer, she argues, is as much part of the ethnographic text as the subjects, who "continue to play an externalizing role in the judgments of others. This is a political fact with which our communications – not least among ourselves – must deal" (Strathern, 1987, p. 279). The reader is invited to look at exemplars to understand their 'content' and 'contexts' (Strathern, 1987, p. 256) in order to produce an interpretation from texts that have legitimate but different instances of enunciation of the field of study, pointing out possible disjunctions – "these are mediated through relationships internal to the text, in the way the writer arranges his [her] ideas" – in the writing style of the field analysed, in ways that are highly relevant to management scholars.

Specifically, we will draw on Strathern's (1987) ideas to analyse Jermier (1985) as an exemplary publication of narrative fiction in the context of management learning to explore disjunction in a field. When using Strathern (1987) to analyse Jermier (1985), the text can be described as the result of intellectual choices that converted a set of perspectives into a *set of statements*, participating in the production of the field of narrative fiction. On the other hand, *statements about* Jermier (1985) can be described as 'modalities', that is, statements about the veracity or positivity of other statements, which add and subtract aspects of the text (check Ducrot & Todorov, 1979; Latour & Woolgar, 1986; Strathern 1987).

Modality

Modality can be explained as a statement about another statement, where 'the speaker' makes a judgement concerning 'another speech' in relation to its enunciation context (cf. Ducrot & Todorov, 1979, p. 303; Latour & Woolgar, 1986, p. 90).

The modalities – statements about statements – that extended Jermier (1985) are grouped into the following types, which:

1 'Deny' Jermier (1985).
2 'Affirm' Jermier (1985).
3 'Relate' to Jermier (1985) to affirm the 'need' for extension of knowledge.
4 'Associate' with Jermier (1985) to produce 'possible' new paths for knowledge.

Modalities 3 and 4 produce deontic operations, indicating what should be done (Ducrot and Todorov, 1979).

Travelling, searching and discovering new approaches

The protagonist of our story is a Brazilian student who grew up between the Open-Air Museum of Inhotim and the Waterfall of Ostras in Brumadinho, Brazil. He wrote an undergraduate thesis at the Federal University of Minas Gerais (UFMG). The topic involved qualitative organizational research about Brumadinho, a place that was razed by the mud from Vale mining's tailing dam in the Brazilian state of Minas Gerais on January 25, 2019. The disaster occurred when the tailings dam at the Córrego do Feijão iron ore mine collapsed. The dam released a mudflow that advanced through the mine's offices, including a cafeteria during lunchtime, devastating houses, farms, inns and roads downstream, killing 270 people. For the thesis, he sought to understand how the massive sea of mud affected the 'emotion' and 'dreams' of its workers. However, he was not sure how to research, describe and analyse 'emotions' and 'dreams', extremely subjective elements of investigation for any scientific field.

The difficulty of collecting and analysing subjective data – such as 'dreams' and 'emotions' – is well known (see Donnelly, Gabriel & Özkazanç-Pan, 2013; Gabriel, 1995; Kara, 2013). Aware of this fact, the student sought to expand his knowledge through an opportunity to gain international academic experience in Australia, where he intended to learn how to collect and analyse subjective data. In Australia, the student attended a public university in Sydney (University), where he took numerous subjects, such as Advanced Management and Organizational Research Methods and Researching Organizations and Management. The former subject was offered by a distinguished professor who had already agreed to be his local supervisor. Accordingly, Researching Organizations and Management was the first subject the student undertook.

In this subject, the students were encouraged to read the book *Doing Exemplary Research* closely, a book written by Frost and Stablein in 1992 as an analysis of the construction of seven 'exemplary' publications. The students had to choose one of these exemplars in the book to defend, expand and criticize in the next class. The professor sought to use these exemplars as manifest lessons in what peers deemed exemplary and why they did so; in addition, there was a latent function, that of honing the students' skills in literature search and crucial review. Later in the subject they would be asked to identify exemplars for their own research and analyse them accordingly. To begin, the professor said: "open the teaching plan of the discipline and check the exemplary publications written in the book." All of them opened, in a synchronized manner, the teaching plan, which is reproduced in the table below:

Teaching plan (excerpt)

The list of official exemplars follows the structure of the prescribed course text: Peter Frost and Ralph Sablein (Eds), *Doing Exemplary Research*, Sage. The book discusses seven exemplary publications. These papers will be available for download from University Online in the 'Subject Documents' Section under Exemplars:

1   Barley, Stephen et al. (1988) Cultures of culture: Academics, practitioners and the pragmatics of normative control, ASQ, 33, 24–60.
2   Gersick, C. J. G. (1988) Time and transition in work teams: Towards a new model of group development, *Academy of Management Review*, 11, 67–80.
3   Meyer, A. D. (1982) Adapting to environmental jolts, ASQ, 27, 515–537.
4   Sutton, R. I. & Rafaeli, A. (1988) Untangling the relationship between displayed emotions and organizational sales: The case of convenience stores, AMJ, 31, 461–487.
5   Jermier, J. (1985) When the sleeper awakes: A short story extending themes in radical organization theory, JOM, 11(2), 67–80.
6   Barron, James N. et al. (1986) War and peace: The evolution of modern personnel administration in U. S. industry, AJS, 92, 350–383.
7   Latham, Gary P. et al. (1988) Resolving scientific disputes by the joint design of crucial experiments by the antagonists:

Applications to the Erez-Latham dispute regarding participation in goal-setting, JAP, 73, 753–772.

In the professor's words:

> Managing a literature review is a demanding task. It is a task that requires not only exhaustiveness but also direction given by an analytic backbone, a narrative. One way of developing a narrative is through establishing exemplary publication. Exemplary publications are works that function theoretically and methodologically as signposts – they help us find our way.
>
> Texts are exemplary in that they both relate to a substantive field of interest and because they enjoy peer esteem as pieces of work that are out of the ordinary in some way, methodologically or theoretically, or in terms of the data they use.

The professor went on to say that "in this subject you will look at authoritatively determined exemplars, critically discuss them, establish similar exemplars for your research efforts, evaluate these and show how they orient your research efforts." The student understood, from the explanation given by the professor, that he needed to find, among the seven chapters inscribed in Frost and Stablein (1992), an exemplar for his research to achieve at least 50 per cent of the subject's total assessment.

Later, at the Centre for Social Innovation and Business, after a meeting of the Discipline Management Group, the student had a first consultation with his supervisor to expose and discuss concerns. After explaining the two environmental catastrophes in Brazil in 2015 and 2019, caused by Samarco and Vale S/A respectively, the student discussed his connection to the *Brumadinho* dam disaster and his idea of studying feelings and emotions in the local context. Recognizing the extremely subjective character of the data that should be collected, the student was anxious about how to do it. The teacher listened and promptly tried to calm him down, saying that by luck, or by chance, one of the seven exemplary publications used to frame the subject being undertaken was precisely about the difficulty of collecting, analysing and expressing highly subjective information, such as theories about social alienation. It was a seminal article from the field of research on narrative fiction, written by John M. Jermier, in 1985, titled "'When the sleeper wakes': a short story extending themes in radical organization theory". In the teacher's understanding, fictional but grounded writing could be used to expose highly subjective data collected in the field.

The student was reticent, however; unaware of this field of research he had intended to use organizational learning to frame the data. The supervisor suggested otherwise; this would be the perfect time to discover and map the potential of the research field in narrative fiction, considering the need to collect, analyse and expose highly subjective data: "take this opportunity to outline and understand this field of research from Jermier (1985)." And he added: "as Bruno Latour teaches us in *Reassembling the Social*, you do not 'frame' anything in doing and writing qualitative research. It is the data that point to the harmonic ways of establishing a dialogue with literature!".

Dazed and confused, the student thanked the professor and left his office with the certainty that, despite his anxieties, the suggestions made by the professor, as his local supervisor, must be given consideration. The student recalled that, in the classroom, the teacher had been clear about what needs to be done, leaving the students to define only how to do it:

> Choose an official exemplar from those in the Frost and Stablein book to defend, extend, and critique at the next meeting. You will identify: (1) citations of the chosen work; (2) extensions of the chosen work by the authors and others; and (3) critiques of the chosen work to see what has been made of it by the literature. You will analyse: How the work in question was possible – what were the assumptions about science, knowledge, etc, that grounded it? You will do these things to develop skills in tracing ideas, their development, critique, and citation, as well as building up skills in the literature review.

To define how to defend, extend and critique an official exemplar from Frost and Stablein (1992), the student thought it would be interesting to use Strathern (1987) to analyse Jermier's (1985) statements as the result of intellectual choices that converted a set of perspectives into a set of statements as well as statements about Jermier (1985) as 'modalities', that is, statements about the veracity or positivity of other statements (see Ducrot & Todorov, 1979; Latour & Woolgar, 1986; Strathern 1987). Hence, he could demonstrate how Jermier (1985) used literature and how his statements were later used. Using Jermier (1985), the student could appreciate the importance of understanding the extent to which an exemplary publication uses the previous literature and the types of uses and interpretations of the literary vision contained in it.

Describing Jermier's (1985) statements – choices, perspectives and utterances

Slightly dishevelled and punctual, the professor came in greeting the class and taking off his scarf. He puts his satchel on the chair, adjusting the table to his height. Patiently, he took off his glasses, turned on the computer and shook his hair. As if he were still listening to the music that was playing in his car, he keeps on moving his head slightly and stomping his right foot. The student remembered that the distinguished professor recently said in an article that his famous theoretical model was not produced deliberately:

> When I drew the model, it looked similar to circuit models I was familiar with from models represented in the handbooks that went with my audio equipment. It was really my love of music, leading to experience with stereo systems, that was the inspiration.

The computer went on and after a few clicks, *My Old School*, a song by Steely Dan, started playing, making everybody comfortable as they waited for the stragglers to the class to arrive. Then, the professor went to one of the three interactive boards in the classroom and tested his pens. He looked at everyone's eyes, smiled and started the class soon after the song stopped: "Greetings everyone!".

After the professor gave a brief introduction about *How to Write*, he said that today everyone would have to present their choice of the exemplary publications to be analysed for the class. First, Katie described Sutton and Rafaeli's (1988) statements. The presentation intrigued the professor as he could see in Katie's speech science in the making. Next, the professor asked the student from Brazil to present his choice, ' "When the Sleeper Wakes"*:* A Short Story Extending Themes in Radical Organization Theory'. The exemplary publication under analysis has parallels with H. G. Well's futuristic novel. Such parallelism is analogous because Mike Armstrong, just as – Graham – the main personality from the book *When the Sleeper Wakes*, awakes from a deep sleep/dream and bumps into a nightmare. Even though the particularities of each story are different, Mike Armstrong's experience – dreaming and awake – is of an alienated life as a worker in a phosphate plant located in Tampa, Florida, marked by complex mechanisms of administrative control.

Jermier's short story is about the two minds of Mike Armstrong, this fictional but experientially representative worker. The dual states of mind/action that "dramatize the existential moments of personal alienation (Laing, 1965) and symbolize the self-contradictory aspects of capitalist systems" (Jermier, 1985, pp. 73–74) are related to dialectical Marxist theory's everyman and critical theory's anti-hero, which are presented through two versions of the ideal type character's work life, namely: the dream (night) and the nightmare (day). Jermier (1985) demonstrated the relevance of his arguments in the article, the student said, through theoretical analysis with a subjectivist method that recovered relevant theoretical concepts, developing implications related to the issues that are recast. Hence, through the short story, Jermier's (1985, p. 79) work could illustrate theoretical viewpoints of critical theory, dialectical Marxism and the self-actualizing worker, exploring alienating consciousness to "depict the effects of problematical organizational events on workers quite differently".

Please, said the professor, tell us a little more about how Jermier (1985) managed to publish such an alternative article, at a time when social sciences and applied social sciences were still marked by paradigmatic studies that were mostly quantitative. The student said that he thought Jermier (1985) was setting his work apart from previous literature adhering to what he called traditional organization theory. The student backed up his statements with multiple data, constituting legitimation. The legitimation cited research that related to critical theory and dialectical Marxism's alternative approaches, which Jermier used to generate an objectivity effect for "concepts of humanistic management that are radically different from traditional organization theory" (Jermier, 1985, p. 79). Not just different but also substantively progressive, since these two approaches recognize "the political-economic context in analysing subjective states and propose macro-level change strategies to eliminate alienation and humanize work (e.g., Jacoby, 1975; Nord, 1977)" (Jermier, 1985, p. 179). Thus, to understand organizational behaviour concerning human meaning-making practices, Jermier (1985) affirmed the viability of using critical theory and dialectical Marxism. Lastly, it is important to point out, said the student, that Jermier's (1985) paper, as a mixed-genre piece, "arose from a strong desire to share difficult insights with a broad audience" (Jermier, 1992, p. 219), doing so in a way that transformed the relationship constructed between the writer and the reader, freeing its readers to interpret a literary text in ways inadmissible within traditional organization theory, in which validity results from the separation of the context of writer, reader and subject.

The professor then thanked the student and explained to the class that Jermier (1985) was published in a special edition of the *Journal of Management* on organizational symbolism (Volume 11, Issue 2, Summer 1985). For Frost (1985), who guest-edited the special issue, it had become imperative to understand organizations from within, through analysis of understandings, meanings and emotions. In the special issue, Jermier (1985) demonstrated the viability of critical theory and dialectical Marxism as practices that could incorporate new accounts of what constituted data. Then, the professor called the next presentation up: "Rosemarie, you are presenting *Cultures of Culture*, is that right?"

Articles using/citing the analysed text – the statements about Jermier (1985)

In the next class, students had to present how their exemplary publications under analysis had been used and critiqued, extended and adapted. The teacher walked into the classroom, settled down, ordered his equipment and again put on a song to lift everyone's spirits as they waited for the rest of the class to arrive from the heavy traffic of the morning rush hour. Fats Waller, 'Your Feet's too Big', this time, with a grainy black and white video of a 1930s movie clip.

When the song was over, the teacher suggested that the presentations begin. The Brazilian student offered to get the day of presentations underway. He started by saying that the work of Jermier (1985) has become a constituent part of several fields. This fact is evident if we consider that 105 other articles referenced the article, according to a survey done in Google Scholar on August 16, 2017: "to analyse the weight of Jermier's work (1985), one must also consider the effects that this knowledge is still producing", he said.

The student discussed the extensions made in three periods: (1) 1985–1995; (2) 1996–2006 and (3), 2001–2017. He analysed the statements – articles, essays, chapters, books – produced about Jermier (1985), constituting a multiple and complex range of modalities (Ducrot & Todorov, 1979), extending its main objectives and issues. The modalities that extended the work of Jermier (1985) were grouped in the following types: those that (1) denied this path to the activity of knowledge; (2) referred to it to affirm their statements; (3) related to it to confirm and/or extend this research approach; and (4) related to it to produce other, alternatives paths, to knowledge.

After presenting the essays that mentioned Jermier (1985) in each of the three periods, the student advised that among the hundred articles citing Jermier (1985), less than 3 per cent of the total (3 out of 90 articles could be analysed as other than citations that merely mentioned the reference in passing) tried to deny the theoretical path proposed by Jermier. For the student, it was not that Jermier (1985) produced exemplary research because a specific book said so (Frost & Stablein,

1992) but because of "its use of earlier literature, inscription devices, documents, and statements as well as [...] subsequent reaction to it" (Latour and Woolgar, 1986, p. 86).

"So, you analysed how Jermier (1985) was used posteriorly, as well as the criticisms made of it." The professor looked down to his notebook to read an annotation. "But what about the field of narrative fiction he draws on and helps establish as a legitimate enterprise for research?" "Yes, right", the student said, looking for the essay in his briefcase. "I thought it would be better to restrict my presentation to the content of the article." In rejoinder, the professor said, "tell me a little more about it; open the essay, read it. Where is the field of narrative fiction at in subsequent research?" Replying, the student says, "It is at the end part, in the discussion topic", opening the text at the correct page. "Let me read it to you."

> From 1985 to 1995, within the symbolic turn (Frost, 1985; Hunt, 1985), an understanding of the uses of narrative fiction was developed and extended. The relationship between the writer and the reader was transformed as emergent forms of representation were offered, allowing non-traditional management academics to write about the subjects' imagination, which is added to the text for the reader to read alternatively. Thus, the reader can learn how to inscribe the subjective experiences of organizational life (fantasy, humour, anger, aesthetics) in the academic text by reading Gabriel (1995) and Phillips (1995). The relationship between the writer and the reader was also transformed to interpret the text being read as a literary work. On the other hand, the texts inscribed within this period show that the relationship constructed between the writer and the subject still depends on the social context of particular and similar organizations so that the research findings can be compared; both authors state that stories and narratives cannot disregard context, meanings or quality descriptions. Lastly, the relationship that is produced between the reader and the subject was broadened, since the writer can now offer enigmatic, contradictory and complex situations of workers in organizational contexts as experiments for the reader, who can choose between modes of subjectivity (subject as a hero, heroic survivor, victim or object of love) that are inscribed and can be observed (Gabriel, 1995), either through a fictional narrative aimed at teaching and learning management, as well as offering aesthetic resources, data or method (Phillips, 1995).
>
> From 1996 to 2006, the relationship that is constructed between writer and reader is still open to dialogue and inspiration; the reader

has the freedom to judge the writer and their text, being inspired to build upon the literary form inscribed in it. Whiteman (2004) argues that the relationship built between the writer of narrative fiction and its readers is based on empathy and curiosity; scientific authority does not guarantee readers' persuasive impact. Rhodes and Brown (2005) reinforce this idea by stating that different writings and different readings made from these emergent writings enact multiple consequences of practical value for scholarship. In this case, Rhodes and Brown (2005), Whiteman (2004) and Taylor (2000) recognize that the ambiguity of fictional narrative is of practical, pragmatic value for scholarship because it facilitates learning of theories which, in turn, can increase the utility and employability of such intellectual constructions. The writers embrace practice as enacting multiple realities. Rhodes and Brown (2005) assume that writing is both a method and a tool for producing realities, involving the reader in a description that presupposes the impossibility of representing the research subject; the responsibility of the writer to the reader and the subject is in regard only to their writing and research practices. Hindmost, the relationship between writer and subject was modified since defending the validity of the fictitious research character becomes necessary with narrative fiction's turn to language. The relationship built between subject and reader for narrative fiction does not necessarily need to account for a social context as the basis for research acquiring valid status. For instance, disjunction is evident throughout the text written by Taylor (2000), including a play at the end of the article. It allows the reader to navigate between the positions and natures of 'capitalist pigs' and 'farmers', as well as between different methods used to circumvent worker and organizational problems, due to organizational change from 'communism' to 'capitalism' in a fictitious world, one in which humans and animals have their voices. In this period, the relationship produced between the writer, reader and subject was transforming due to aesthetic theorizing, challenging and responding to limits imposed on scientific representations by being reflexive, pragmatic and ethical, using research findings as guidelines for dealing with issues of responsibility in writing about organizations.

From 2007 to 2017, collaborative and hybrid writing styles emerged as possibilities, linking up more intensely with ideas current in symmetrical anthropology, stressing that organizations are sociomaterial-semiotic constructions. Writing is enacted as an emancipatory and democratic practice either through theatre or the construction of new concepts; new literary genres, notions and ideas are proposed for thinking about organizational research and theory from a postmodern perspective. Accordingly, the ordering and disciplining function of writing is highlighted and representations about organizations and organizational workers are made without distinction between fiction and fact. The writer context is still part of the subject context, allowing readers to inquire into the modes of writing narrative fiction. However, more strongly, the subjects' power to judge others (see Strathern, 1987) became part of writing narrative fiction. As writer, reader and subject become part of the research, each can judge the research (and its researchers) (Strathern, 1987; Warren, 2008). Social sciences as well as applied social sciences, such as organization and management studies, no longer excludes narrative fiction.

"Sure, it is a partial description", said the student, using shorthand to refer to the substantive field of organization and management theory. He halted for a moment, searching for something in the essay.

Seminal researchers on the subject are located outside of the present research network of studies connecting fiction and fact as a broader subject, going beyond Jermier (1985) and anything(one) else. Still, the web of studies being traced is partial but also connected if we consider what Strathern (2005) teaches us.

The professor stood up and asked the student to sit down.

In a couple of weeks, I am going to send you my assessment of the paper. I can tell you one thing, though: if your text, besides analysing Jermier (1985) critically, says something about the field of narrative fiction, you have to change the title. Moreover, you provided evidence that the negations, assertions and extensions of Jermier's statements offer new insights for future research. Do these negations, affirmations, and extensions lead to theory development in any way?"

Replying, the student again read from his text.

Adopting the post-structuralist idea that a theory must challenge internal contexts/conventions of scholarship and transform the social context/life of investigators (see Strathern 1987), the ideas inscribed in this literature review article will only lead to theory development if further investigations elaborate and transform it, pluralizing learning and official texts.

Looking up from his notes to the professor's gaze, he asked, "Do you agree with this definition of organization theory development?"
The professor replied:

Sounds reasonable to me. We may continue with this discussion later on. You ended up enjoying Jermier (1985), is that not so? I am curious to know how you will link up with Jermier (1985) to collect subjective data and analyse 'dreams' and 'emotions'.

Then he gathered some papers from the front of the room and went back to sit with the students to watch the next presentation. "These are notoriously difficult to access other than through accounts and attributions, respectively. Thank you. Who is coming up next?"

Final considerations

The student had produced a literature review to develop a theory of narrative fiction by describing (1) Jermier's (1985) statements and (2) statements about Jermier (1985). Hence, our character outlined an empirical method with which to understand the practice of building substantive knowledge. We suggest that the empirical method used can be understood as a fruitful and interesting initiative which, although mediated by the selection of a certain text and limited to the objective conditions imposed by that very choice, can be used more widely. Therefore, the controversies surrounding the debate are not over. The present chapter opens possibilities for future studies that use the empirical method for the analysis of other texts or contexts to produce further accounts and theoretical development.

The account in this chapter recalls a classroom use of Frost and Stablein's (1992) *Doing Exemplary Research*. The book works well, albeit being dated now, with the passing years, for students and instructors in Organization and Management Studies. However, the methods structuring it can be applied anywhere. We suggest that it is easy for instructors to form a list of exemplars in any discipline and build a method based on exemplary research in their field. Follow these steps:

1   Do a small survey with colleagues and graduate students in the discipline in which you work in your institution.

2   Share the list with a broader set of colleagues known from conferences and other institutions. Frame a survey instrument with three columns beside each posited exemplar:

Endorse	Reject	Why?

3   Using the data generated and your discretion, trim the list generated to about six or seven papers with each paper representing a distinct methodological approach. You now have the basis for a course introducing students in your discipline area to exemplary research.

Questions

1   It is one thing to suggest how the method should be understood and used, another is to comprehend and be persuaded by the need to use the method inscribed in the story. After reading our research-based narrative fiction, what do you think are the take-aways from this story?
2   What has the story added to your understanding about reviewing the literature to develop organization theory today?
3   How does the story you have just read resonate with your experiences in reviewing the literature?
4   What have you learnt from the experience of each of the characters and how can you bring it to your research practice and experience of reviewing the literature to develop theory?

Next, there are some reflective questions to plan the literature review of your qualitative research. There is also a table indicating complementary literature.

Reflective issues

It is important to think about the following: what do you need to keep in mind to write the literature review for your research if you are to develop theory? Reflexively, take some time to remember a few important points before starting to review the literature:

• In relation with your fieldwork experience, projected or started already, did you manage to identify one or more exemplary publications for your research as a way of defining the field in question?

- If so, have you already analysed the *exemplary publication's statements* and *statements about the exemplary publication*?
- Have you started to describe the *exemplary publication's statements* and the *statements about it* through narrative, time bracketing and visual mapping strategies (see Langley, 1999; Pratt, 2009) to produce a theorized literature review?

Complementary readings

This chapter addresses how researchers can write the literature review of a qualitative research from an exemplary publication. As particular themes could not be analysed with greater intensity, Table 2 summarizes complementary readings to aid systematic literature review.

Table 2 Complementary readings on literature review

Related methodological themes	Comments	Reading suggestions
Qualitative research	Excellent work that will help you in engaging in qualitative research	Cassell and Sumon (2004), Mason (1997), Silverman (2020, 2022), Charmaz (2014)
Literary reviews	Texts that allow you to make sense of past investigations and develop, extend and refine organization theory. These texts will help you map emergent research topics and introduce you to novel forms of representing, writing and theorizing. Doing this will enable you to place your qualitative research in a broader context.	Blaxter, Hughes and Tight (1996), Burton (2000), Cornelissen, Höllerer and Seidl (2021), Hart (1998), Sandberg and Alvesson (2021)
Textual analysis	Methods of textual analysis can be used to review literature to develop theory. Analysis of the content and structure of texts allows us to understand how these are constructed and the scientific fields to which they contribute.	Barthes (1977), Derrida (1974), Latour and Woolgar (1986), McKee (2003), and Rose (2001a, 2001b 2001c)

(*continued*)

Table 2 Cont.

Related methodological themes	Comments	Reading suggestions
Content analysis	Content analysis of selected texts is used to highlight their themes and concepts. Content analysis considers the frequency of repetition of words and/or terms. Frequency analysis of scientific texts informs us about those meanings and ideas repeatedly used in the text.	Jupp (2006), Rose (2001a), Ryan and Bernard (2003)
Citation context analysis	Analysis of citations addresses the scholarly impact of seminal texts and influential authors, providing an emergent frame for reviewing the literature.	Anderson and Lemken (2019), Anderson and Sun (2010), Lounsbury and Carberry (2005)
Intertextuality	Intertextuality refers to the embeddedness of a text (or image) in a context. Intertextual analysis seeks to show how the text in question defers to, refers to and opposes other texts. Using intertextual analysis, the researcher can demonstrate knowledge of the relation of a given text to other equally relevant texts.	Bertens (2001), Rose (2001c)

Source: Prepared by the *authors*.

Note

1   The Brazilian student and the Australian professor, respectively.

References

Anderson, M. H. & Lemken, R. K. (2019). An empirical assessment of the influence of March and Simon's *Organizations*: The realized contribution and unfulfilled promise of a masterpiece. *Journal of Management Studies*, 56, 1537–1569.

Anderson, M. H. & Lemken, R. K. (2020). Citation context analysis as a method for conducting rigorous and impactful literature reviews. *Organizational Research Methods*, doi: 10.1177/1094428120969905.

Anderson, M. H. & Sun, P. Y. T. (2010). Examining our collective memory of an organizational memory classic: What have scholars retrieved from Walsh and Ungson (1991)? *Management Learning*, 41, 131–145.

Barthes, R. ([1961–73] 1977). *Images–music–text*. London: Fontana.

Baumeister, R. F. & Leary, M. R. (1997). Writing narrative literature reviews. *Review of General Psychology*, 1, 311–320.

Bertens, H. (2001). *Literary theory: The basics*. London: Routledge.

Blaxter, L., Hughes, C. & Tight, M. (1996). *How to research*. Milton Keynes: Open University Press.

Breslin, D., Gatrell, C. & Bailey, K. (2020). Developing insights through reviews: Reflecting on the 20th anniversary of the *International Journal of Management Reviews*. *International Journal of Management Reviews*, 22(1), 3–9.

Burton, D. (2000). Using literature to support research. In Burton, D. (Ed.), *Research training for social scientists: A handbook for postgraduate researchers* (pp. 137–152). London: Sage.

Cassell, C. & Sumon, G. (2004). *Essential guide to qualitative methods*. London: Sage.

Charmaz, K. (2014). *Constructing grounded theory*. London: Sage.

Cornelissen, J., Höllerer, M. A. & Seidl, D. (2021). What theory is and can be: Forms of theorizing in organizational scholarship. *Organization Theory*, 2(3), 1–19.

Cropanzano, R. (2009). Writing non-empirical articles for journal of management: General thoughts and suggestions. *Journal of Management*, 35(6), 1304–1311.

Denyer, D. & Tranfield, D. (2009). Producing a systematic review. In Buchanan, D. & Bryman, A. (Eds), *The Sage handbook of organizational research methods* (pp. 671–689). London: Sage.

Derrida, J. (1974). *Of grammatology* (G. C. Spivak, Trans.). Baltimore, MD: Johns Hopkins University Press (original work published in 1967).

Donnelly, P. F., Gabriel, Y. & Özkazanç-Pan, B. (2013). Untold stories of the field and beyond: Narrating the chaos. *Qualitative Research in Organizations and Management: An International Journal*, 8, 4–15.

Ducrot, O. & Todorov, T. (1979). *Encyclopedic dictionary of the sciences of language* (C. Porter, Trans.). Baltimore, MD: The Johns Hopkins University Press (Original: *Dictionnaire encyclopedie des sciences du langage*, Paris, 1973).

Frazer, J. G. (1825). *The golden bough*. The Project Gutenberg EBook, http://markfoster.net/rn/the_golden_bough.pdf, accessed 09.07.2020.

Frost, P. J. (1985). Special issue on organizational symbolism. *Journal of Management*, 11(2), 5–9.

Frost, P. J. & Stablein, R. E. (Eds). (1992). *Doing exemplary research*. London: Sage.

Gabriel, Y. (1995). The unmanaged organization: Stories, fantasies and subjectivity. *Organization Studies*, 16(3), 477–501.

Gatrell, C. & Breslin, D. (2017). Editors' statement. *International Journal of Management Reviews*, 19(1), 1–3.

Hart, C. (1998). *Doing a literature review*. London: Sage.

Hunt, J. (1985). Comments from the editor. *Journal of Management*, 11(2), 4–4.

Jermier, J. M. (1985). 'When the sleeper wakes': A short story extending themes in radical organization theory. *Journal of Management*, 11(2), 67–80.

Jermier, J. M. (1992) Literary methods and organization science: Reflection on 'when the sleeper wakes'. In Frost, P. and Stablein, R. (Eds), *Doing exemplary research* (pp. 210–226). Newbury Park, CA: Sage.

Jones, O. & Gatrell, C. (2014). The future of writing and reviewing for IJMR. *International Journal of Management Reviews*, 16(3), 249–264.

Jupp, V. (2006). *The Sage dictionary of social research methods*. London: Sage.

Kara, H. (2013). It's hard to tell how research feels: Using fiction to enhance academic research and writing. *Qualitative Research in Organizations and Management: An International Journal*, 8(1), 70–84.

Kilduff, M. (2006). Editor's comments: Publishing theory. *Academy of Management Review*, 31(2), 252–255.

Kunisch, S., Menz, M., Bartunek, J. M., Cardinal, L. B. & Denyer, D. (2018). Feature topic at organizational research methods: how to conduct rigorous and impactful literature reviews? *Organizational Research Methods*, 21(3), 519–523.

Laing, R. D. (1965). *The divided self*. London: Penguin Books.

Langley, A. (1999). Strategies for theorizing from process data. *Academy of Management review*, 24(4), 691–710.

Latour, B., & Woolgar, S. (1986). *Laboratory life*. London: Sage.

Lounsbury, M. & Carberry, E. J. (2005). From king to court jester? Weber's fall from grace in organizational theory. *Organization Studies*, 26, 501–525.

Mason, J. (1997). *Qualitative researching*. London: Sage.

McKee, A. (2003). *Textual analysis: A beginner's guide*. London: Sage.

Phillips, N. (1995). Telling organizational tales: On the role of narrative fiction in the study of organizations. *Organization Studies*, 16(4), 625–649.

Post, C., Sarala, R., Gatrell, C. and Prescott, J. E. (2020). Advancing theory with review articles. *Journal of Management Studies*, 57(2), 351–376.

Rhodes, C. & Brown, A. D. (2005). Writing responsibly: Narrative fiction and organization studies. *Organization*, 12(4), 467–491.

Rose, G. (2001a). Content analysis: Counting what you (think you) see. In *An introduction to the interpretation of visual materials* (pp. 59–74). London: Sage.

Rose, G. (2001b). Discourse analysis: Text, intertextuality, context. In *An introduction to the interpretation of visual materials* (pp. 135–163). London: Sage.

Rose, G. (2001c). Semiology. In *An introduction to the interpretation of visual materials* (pp. 69–99). London: Sage.

Ryan, G. W. & Bernard, R. (2003). Techniques to identify themes. *Field Methods* 15(1), 85–109.

Sandberg, J. & Alvesson, M. (2021). Meanings of theory: Clarifying theory through typification. *Journal of Management Studies*, 58(2), 487–516.

Silverman, D. (Ed.). (2020). *Qualitative research*. London: Sage.

Silverman, D. (2022). *Doing qualitative research: A practical handbook*. London: Sage.

Snyder, H. (2019). Literature review as a research methodology: An overview and guidelines. *Journal of Business Research*, 104, 333–339.

Strathern, M. (1987). Out of context. *Current Anthropology*, 28(3), 251–281.

Strathern, M. (2005). *Partial connections*. Altamira: Rowman.

Suddaby, R., Hardy, C. & Huy, Q. N. (2011). Introduction to special topic forum: Where are the new theories of organization? *Academy of Management Review*, 36(2), 236–246.

Sutton, R. I. & Rafaeli, A. (1988) "Untangling the relationship between displayed emotions and organizational sales: The case of convenience stores", *Academy of Management Journal*, 31, 461–487.

Taylor, S. S. (2000). Aesthetic knowledge in academia: Capitalist pigs at the academy of management. *Journal of Management Inquiry*, 9(3), 304–328.

Torraco, R. J. (2005). Writing integrative literature reviews: Guidelines and examples. *Human Resource Development Review*, 4, 356–367.

Torraco, R. J. (2016). Writing integrative literature reviews: Using the past and present to explore the future. *Human Resource Development Review*, 15(4), 404–428.

Van Maanen, J., Sørensen, J. B. & Mitchell, T. R. (2007). The interplay between theory and method. *Academy of Management Review*, 32(4), 1145–1154.

Vickers, M. H. (2010). The creation of fiction to share other truths and different viewpoints: A creative journey and an interpretive process. *Qualitative Inquiry*, 16(7), 556–565.

Vickers, M. H. (2011). Taking a compassionate turn for workers with multiple sclerosis (MS): Towards the facilitation of management learning. *Management Learning*, 42(1), 49–65.

Vickers, M. H. (2015). Stories, disability, and 'dirty' workers: Creative writing to go beyond too few words. *Journal of Management Inquiry*, 24(1), 82–89.

Warren, S. (2008). Empirical challenges in organizational aesthetics research: Towards a sensual methodology. *Organization Studies*, 29(4), 559–580.

Webster, J. & Watson, R. T. (2002). Analyzing the past to prepare for the future: Writing a literature review. *MIS Quarterly*, 26(2), xiii–xxiii.

Weick, K. E. (1989). Theory construction as disciplined imagination. *Academy of Management Review*, 14(4), 516–531.

Whiteman, G. (2004). Why are we talking inside? Reflecting on traditional ecological knowledge (TEK) and management research. *Journal of Management Inquiry*, 13(3), 261–277.

Whiteman, G. & Phillips, N. (2008). The role of narrative fiction and semi-fiction in organization studies. In Barry, D. & Hansen, H. (Eds), *New approaches in management and organization* (pp. 288–299). Los Angeles, CA: Sage.

3 Collecting and analysing data from a cartography of controversies

César Tureta, Bruno Luiz Américo and Stewart Clegg

Keywords: Cartography of Controversies; Qualitative Research; Data collection; Data analysis; Creative writing; Paradigm of a screenplay; Ethnographic fiction.

Expected learning outcomes

At the end of the chapter, readers will be able to:

- Recognize what constitute controversies.
- Apply criteria for choosing controversies and their implications for research practice.
- Understand how to use five focal points to guide data analysis.
- Appreciate the importance for analysis of visual representation of controversies.
- Design qualitative research based on a cartography of controversies.
- Frame data analysis presenting research findings using creative writing.

Introduction

This chapter presents a cartography of controversies (Venturini, 2010a,b) as a guide for collecting and analysing qualitative data. We present a practical guide for researchers interested in investigating a situation and topics characterized by disagreements and conflicts. Tensions and different points of view about issues reveal the limits of that which is taken-for-granted by different interests. Despite being a powerful tool for inquiry into several practices (Venturini, 2010 a,b; Tureta, Américo

DOI: 10.4324/9781003198161-4

& Clegg, 2021a,b), controversy analysis remains underexplored as a method. Recently, some scholars have used this approach in qualitative research to investigate the nature of objects in organizational processes (Hussenot & Missonier, 2010), the role of numbers in contributing and mediating different forms of board governance (Michaud, 2014) and the enactment of the past and its history in the implementation of a contract between a labour services company and a public university hospital (Tureta, Américo & Clegg, 2021b). By explaining controversy analysis practically, we seek to inspire further use of this approach.

In addition to addressing controversy analysis, we relate it to creative writing (Vickers, 2010, 2015). More specifically, we draw on Watson's (2000) notion of ethnographic fiction. Adopting this approach allows researchers to use their creativity more freely and explore a broader range of events and insights based on fieldwork experience (Watson, 2000). Doing so, the researcher provides a smoother narrative and opens "room for the reader to enter into the lifeworld constructed by the text" (Phillips, 1995, p. 628), leading to engagement with the story, aiding readers' sensemaking (Savage, Cornelissen & Franck, 2018). Creative writing facilitates the inclusion of different viewpoints in the text (Phillips, 1995) and questions the status of authorized accounts (Pick, 2017). Creative writing aligns with controversy analysis in its aim to multiply actors' points of view and in questioning how phenomena are performed, offering a practical guide for researching.

Qualitative research frees the researcher from a priori conceptual straightjackets (Jarzabkowski, Langley and Nigam, 2021). These can be imposed by hypothesis testing premised on researchers' frames for doing fieldwork and analysing data. In contrast, it poses a conversation between the practical consciousness of the actors in the field with the theoretical consciousness that the researcher uses to engage with those actors and their artefacts. So, our guide should not be viewed as a rigid process but as a path that can take new and different directions, depending on the aim of the research.

This chapter is structured as follows. First, we present how to collect data based on a cartography of controversies. We clarify what controversies are and suggest four criteria that researchers may use in choosing controversies and explain their implications for research practice. Five focal points, with respective questions, are suggested in defining data collection protocols. We provide some tips concerning each of the five focal points. Next, we describe the data analysis process, divided into three moments. First, the five focal points are used as a grid for data analysis; how to analyse data in each element of the grid is explained. Next, we create a visual representation of the controversy mapping to facilitate an understanding of the issue at stake. Finally, we draw on the paradigm of a screenplay elaborated by the screenwriter, Syd Field, to frame the story we tell as ethnographic fiction. We illustrate the use of ethnographic writing using data collected and analysed from research conducted in a samba school in Brazil. Then, we show the creative writing created during the data analysis process. The story is divided into three Acts based on the paradigm of a screenplay: Act I is the set-up; Act II is the confrontation; Act III is the resolution. Finally, we present some considerations, reflective issues, as well as complementary readings.

Collecting data

Doing research focused on the cartography of controversy requires multiple sources of data (Venturini, 2010a). Researchers must seek access to as many data sources as possible, from observations to interviews, through documents and photos, online data when available, as well as shadowing actors and closely observing practices at work. Finding controversies that are worth investigating is a great aid to focusing on data collection and analysis.

What are controversies?

A controversy irrupts when various actors disagree about a specific issue that previously appeared to have been taken for granted but becomes questioned and debated (Venturini, 2010a), when non-issues become issues either in specific situation, such as meetings, or in subsequent commentary and reflection on these. When states of affairs become issuable, the status quo is disturbed (Hussenot & Missonier, 2010); the grounds underlying how an activity is managed (Hussenot, 2014) as well as the tacit rules constituting it, become more evident. Challenges to taken-for-granted assumptions reveal the dynamics of interaction (Venturini, 2010a). Controversy should not be confused with one-off conflicts that are ordinary events in everyday life, although conflicts may trigger controversies when they become snowball issues (Hussenot, 2008). Controversies reveal the fissures and tensions, as well as the paradoxes, that are inscribed in society.

To investigate a controversy, the researcher should identify the representation of the interests and divergent points of view at stake, whether these representations are enacted discursively by people or are embedded in aspects of artefactual actants (Venturini, 2010b). It is important to follow actors (Latour, 2005) in doing fieldwork, all the while treating humans and non-human actants symmetrically (Law, 1994). In Table 3, we summarize what controversies are and explain the meaning of each aspect that comprises them.

Keeping these points in mind is helpful for researchers when starting fieldwork and identifying a controversy that is worth investigating and exploring. Most of the data collection and analysis techniques that we shall discuss are grounded in Venturini (2010a,b), Venturini, Ricci, Mauri, Kimbell and Meunier (2015), as well as Tureta, Américo and Clegg (2021a,b). Next, we will briefly present an approach to the cartography of controversies before writing the story. We will present four criteria for researchers choosing controversies during the data collection

Table 3 Aspects of a controversy

Controversies are...	What does it mean?
1 Heterogenous	From managers and employees to technologies and artistic products, controversies can be triggered, developed and associated with human actors and non-human actants.
2 Dynamic	Emergent controversies reveal the precariousness of the social contracts and implicit understandings that apparently stabilize relations between actors, displaying the hidden dynamic of interactions. Breaches of the underlying rules constituting taken-for-granted accords reveal the constitutive and preferential situational rules in practice.
3 Reduction-resistant	A disputed issue may cause actors to disagree about anything, leading to a snowballing process. Controversies create space for multiple questions.
4 Debated	As actors question a taken-for-granted issue, controversies give rise to debate around an activity or process in which 'what is to be done?' is at issue. Once issues are enacted, increased numbers of actors and objects become enrolled in debate.
5 Conflictual	Controversies produce the clash of conflicting words and worlds, differences in points of view. In such situations, actors cannot ignore each other. Even trivial issues may produce serious quarrels. As actors are not equals, any controversy can only be stabilized through power relations that may involve any or all or a mixture of actors or objects having 'power over', affording 'power to' others made able to make a difference or creating enhanced 'power with' others.

Source: Adapted from Venturini (2010a).

process. These criteria should not be viewed as exhaustive but as a starting point for fieldwork investigation.

Choosing a controversy

While Venturini (2010a) and Hussenot (2014) recommend that researchers focus on present, 'hot', public and restricted controversy, Tureta, Américo and Clegg (2021a) recommend that researchers can also seek out past, 'cold' and underground controversies as well as evident and pervasive controversies, taking a broad and flexible view of the five criteria. Depending on the phenomenon under analysis, investigation may uncover power relations occluding the social realities being constructed that prevent researchers from identifying hidden but relevant issues in context. Tureta, Américo and Clegg (2021a) argue that:

a *Past* controversies may have been resolved because divergent voices were silenced. The resolution of a controversy could always have been otherwise.
b *Cold* controversies may become interesting as new points of view are raised and prior agreements are no longer taken for granted.
c *Underground* controversies may have been hidden because of the temporary stabilization of power relations that cover them in naturalized institutional structures.
d *Boundless* controversies can be investigated as the researcher follows the actor networks entangled in them.

In alignment with Tureta, Américo and Clegg (2021a), Table 4 shows the four criteria for choosing controversies and their implications for research practice.

The main idea is to trace connections between different actors involved in controversies. Tureta, Américo and Clegg (2021b) developed a method for studying processes of the past as organizational history through analyses of controversy. We have adapted the method to investigate any type of controversy. Table 5 provides some questions that research may use to guide data collection processes. The focal points are the building blocks for collecting data on controversies. These focal points are especially relevant because they help in the data analysis process, providing guidelines for organizing fieldwork materials and mapping controversies.

Table 4 Criteria for choosing controversies

Criteria	Implications for research practice
1 Embrace present and past controversies	*Present* Salient and unresolved issues are easy to observe and the researcher can follow such controversy as it develops. The (human and non-human) elements of the controversy tend to be more readily available to researchers. Current debates in social media are helpful in mapping present controversies. *Past* Expose what is taken for granted as historical data. The status of any controversy is never definitive, even though power relations may temporarily close controversies. The researcher needs to delve into the past to bring controversies back to life through searching documents and archives, using what is gleaned from these as prompts and frames for present inquiry.
2 Embrace hot and cold controversies	*Hot* Heated debates display the social in its most dynamic form as the conflicts at stake are evidently surfaced. As a result, actors' performativity, its meanings and emotions are more vivid and can be captured during observations. *Cold* A supposedly cold controversy may reveal that lack of debate is the consequence of oppressed actors and issues. Actors' performativity, its meanings and emotions, may be suppressed and hidden in everyday situations. Researchers should follow closely the traces left by the actors to identify any element capable of activating supposedly cold controversy.
3 Embrace public and underground controversies	*Public* Public debates on a specific issue create opportunities to identify the actors and their points of view clearly. Hence, the actor's actions and discourse can be followed closely. *Underground* Expose the politics and power relations masked by burying controversies, covering them with naturalized social relationships and established institutional structures.
4 Beware of boundless controversies	*Boundlessness* Researchers should beware of resource availability as following boundless controversies can be costly. Focus on the actors, both those that make a difference in debates as well as mapping the traces left by overlooked or ignored voices; those not consulted, those marginalized or treated as less significant others.

Source: Adapted from Venturini (2010a) and Tureta, Américo and Clegg (2021a).

Table 5 Protocol for collecting data

Focal points	Questions	Tips for researchers
Sampling: identify the controversies related to the phenomenon under analyses.	*What* are the types of controversies?	*Identify what kind of controversy you are studying.* Controversies can be of various types: technical, economic, cultural, social, aesthetics, legal and so on. It is relevant to identify their types to facilitate following their unfolding and collecting suitable data.
	When do they occur?	*Be attentive to past controversies.* Although current controversies are easy to identify, researchers should also consider those in the past, as they may reveal a continuous and unresolved conflict that remains in the present.
Scanning: map actors involved in the controversies.	*Who* and *what* is involved in the controversies?	*Consider all kinds of actors.* Symmetry is important in collecting data as controversies may involve both humans and non-humans. From managers, employees, CEOs and activists to technologies, artefacts and spaces, different kinds of actors, viewpoints and actants should be considered when collecting data.
Tracing: draw the process of resolving conflicts.	*How* do actors engage in conflicts resolution?	*Follow the traces of conflicts.* Conflicts leave behind traces of their life in the shape of material such as a documents or fragments of stories to be told. As the researcher comes to know who and what is involved in the controversies, following disagreements will be useful in collecting evidence of the conflict resolution process.
Labelling: analyse the politics of controversies.	*Why* are the actors involved in controversies?	*Inspect power relations.* All actors have interests and invest efforts and resources in persuading others. Some are influential and can shape controversies according to their needs. Identify who values what and who has access to what is valued and who denies that access.

Table 5 Cont.

Focal points	Questions	Tips for researchers
Describing: identify the reality being performed by actors.	*Which* reality is performed by actors?	*Reality is multiple.* Reality is not singular but multiple. Sometimes realities conflict, sometimes they overlap. Actors' practices can enact both visible and less visible realities. The researcher should be attentive to the different practices that actors use to perform realities.

Source: Adapted from Tureta, Américo and Clegg (2021b).

Analysing data

The source of the data

The material used to illustrate the data analysis is from a study conducted in a first division samba school in São Paulo city, Brazil, called here Sasc. The carnival cycle studied was the year 2009–10. Every year, the samba schools (*Escola de samba*; social clubs united by samba and embedded in community, sometimes as social movements) compete in a contest that will define the champion. A samba school can be defined as a non-profit cultural and leisure organization whose main objective is to parade in the carnival, a competitive event (Goldwasser, 1975). The parade of the samba schools in São Paulo is the second largest festival of this kind in Brazilian carnival. It is surpassed only by the parade that occurs in Rio de Janeiro in size and in participation in the streets by that of Salvador, Bahia (Clegg, 2000).

Competition has been increasing recently, demanding greater aesthetic performance during the parade day by the drummers, dancers and followers (Júlio & Tureta, 2018). Competitive pressure on samba schools' members creates innovations in performance with which to enchant the jurors and the audience. The hard work required to be the champion leads to several controversies as each school and its community shape its presentation for the day of the parade (Tureta & Américo 2020). So, a samba school is a rich place in which to investigate controversies.

Sasc is one of the oldest and most traditional samba schools in the city of São Paulo. It was founded in 1930 and has been a carnival champion several times. The data used in creating analysis and illustrations in writing the story are drawn from observation of the work of Sasc's *harmonia* team, those responsible for the floats and the management of the shed where the floats are built. The *harmonia* team designs the overall synergy and level of synchronization between the different elements of the parade. Specifically, *harmonia* depends on the coordination between the *passistas* (the samba dancers for each school), the *bateria* (or the team made up of hundreds of percussionists) and the chanting of the samba song by the school.

Floats are the most visible part of a samba school during the parade. On the day of the parade, there is an expectation concerning their size, beauty, colours, movement, sounds and all the aesthetic elements contained in them. The audience always expects to be surprised by something new in the floats. It is because of this expectation about the floats, that the Sasc board is quite demanding of the *harmonia* coordinators of the team. These demands give rise to many controversies during the process of producing the allegories that the float represents.

The first author of this chapter gained access to the various places where the carnival production took place. The observation period lasted six months, during which he took field notes. Over this period, he took part in meetings of the *harmonia* team, attended rehearsals at the samba school's hall, visited its shed where the float is made up, attended technical rehearsals at the Sambadrome[1] and was present during the movement of the floats from the shed to the Sambadrome. Moreover, he paraded as a member of the *alegoria*[2] team. He conducted interviews, took pictures, got access to the samba school documents and emails of the *harmonia* team. He also watched the Sasc's parade through videos on YouTube after the carnival competition.

To analyse the data, we identified the research material that presented evidence and information about the controversies in the production of the floats of the Sasc samba school. Doing this allowed an overview of the main issues at stake. Next, we developed the data analysis in three major moments.

First moment

The first moment was divided into the five stages represented by the focal points in Table 5a. It is worth noting that these stages are not linear because analysing controversies requires researchers to move back and forth between sampling and data collection and analysis constantly (Venturini et al., 2015). Furthermore, the stages can overlap.

In the first stage, *sampling*, we focused our analysis on disagreements that led to snowballing issues to identify a controversy that was not just a one-off conflict. We identified *what* types of heated controversies were at stake: these were technical and aesthetic. Next, we made constant comparisons between many different points of view of the actors involved in the controversies. This allowed us to pinpoint *when* controversies occurred. Technical and aesthetic disagreements were a current issue during the production of the float but also an unresolved issue from the past remembered by actors all the time. For a summary of the first stage, see Table 5a.

Scanning the data was the second stage. We clustered the actors whose participation made some difference to others' actions during the debates. We mapped *who* and *what* was involved in the controversies: humans (e.g., *harmonia* team and board) and non-humans (e.g., floats). To do so, we used the three parameters suggested by Venturini (2010b): representativeness, influence and interest. These parameters consider the viewpoints of the actors and are helpful in delimiting the scope of actors analysed. A *representative* viewpoint has substantial support from various actors who share similar arguments. The statements made by this person or group deserve the researcher's attention. An *influence* viewpoint affects the actions of other actors. While controversy occurs, various actors will try to assume influential positions that shape the controversies. In this sense, some viewpoints will have more influence than others. *Interest* is related to viewpoints that are marginalized. Minorities' viewpoints should be included in

Table 5a Stage 1: Sampling

Focal point	Questions	Example of empirical findings
Sampling: identify the controversies related to the phenomena under analysis.	What are the types of controversies?	*Technical* (e.g., the structure of floats is not finished; the production practice of floats needs to be revised).
		Aesthetics (e.g., the beauty and size of floats are the board's focus; they must perform an amazing and impactful parade).
	When do they occur?	*Present* During the floats productions.
		Past They also occurred in past carnival productions and were remembered by the present actors.

Table 5b Stage 2: Scanning

Focal point	Question	Example of empirical findings
Scanning: map the actors involved in the controversies	Who and what is involved in the controversies?	*Who* Humans (e.g., *harmonia* team and board).
		What Non-humans (e.g., floats).
		Viewpoints Representative: *harmonia* coordinator Influence: carnival director Interest: members of the *harmonia* team

the analysis because they offer different perspectives and question what is usually taken-for-granted. For a summary of the second stage, see Table 5b.

Once we identified the actors debating the floats' problems, we could *trace* their actions and draw the process they used to negotiate their interests. We sought to understand *how* the actors engaged in conflict resolution at this stage. Specifically, we focused on the taken-for-granted practices of floats' production that were questioned by the *harmonia* team (marginal viewpoints) as well as who supported the *harmonia* coordinator's actions (influential viewpoint). We also analysed the responses provided by the board (influence viewpoint). By tracing the actors' actions, we found that the board tried to persuade the *harmonia* team about the lack of resources and that the *harmonia* team improvised solutions for problems that arose with the production of the floats to accomplish their project. For a summary of the third stage, see Table 5c.

Labelling each actors' positions in the debates allowed us to analyse the politics of controversies. To do so, we inspected power relations between actors (board and *harmonia* coordinator), influential positions (carnival director) and marginalized viewpoints (members of the *harmonia* team). As a result of this process, the reasons *why* actors invested efforts in struggling around controversial issues became visible. For example, the board's project was to deliver an unforgettable parade that showed the majesty and beauty of the samba school. The *harmonia* team was interested in providing safety for all the crowd who would parade in the Sambadrome. For a summary of the fourth stage, see Table 5d.

In stage 5, we linked the other focal points to understand and describe which organizational realities were performed by actors involved in the

Table 5c Stage 3: Tracing

Focal point	Question	Example of empirical findings
Tracing: draw the process of resolving conflicts	How do actors engage in conflicts' resolution?	The board tried to *persuade* the *harmonia* team about the lack of resources. The *harmonia* team *improvised* solutions for problems with the floats and accomplished the project.

Table 5d Stage 4: Labelling

Focal point	Question	Example of empirical findings
Labelling: analyse the politics of controversies	Why are the actors involved in controversies?	The board wants to provide an aesthetically *amazing* and *spectacular* show. The *harmonia* team wants to guarantee the *safety* and *proper functioning* of the floats.

Table 5e Stage 5: Describing

Focal point	Question	Example of empirical findings
Describing: identify the reality being performed by actors.	Which organizational reality is performed by actors?	Two overlapping realities: 1 Aesthetics aspects come first; technical issues are details. 2 Beauty cannot be produced without hidden technical details; aesthetics and technical issues should be balanced.

controversies. At this stage of the analysis, it was clear to us what the processual traces were behind the actors' actions and the controversies at stake. These traces allowed us to identify two overlapping realities in the carnival's production for this school. On the one hand, the board's practices created a reality in which the aesthetic aspects should be the priority in the production of the float, considering technical issues as only details that the *harmonia* team can handle. On the other hand, the practices of the *harmonia* team produced a reality in which the aesthetic dimension of the floats could only perform well in the parade if their technical issues were taken seriously. This final stage set the ground for the next moment of the analysis. For a summary of the fifth stage, see Table 5e.

Second moment

In the second moment, aiming to clarify the controversy mapping, we produced a visual representation of the issues around the production of the float (see Figure 1). This representation simplifies the whole dynamic process involved in the controversies and is not intended to be a complete map of their unfolding.

As stated by Venturini (2010b, p. 797), "to be of any use, social maps have to be less confused and convoluted than collective disputes. They cannot just mirror the complexity of controversies: they have to make such complexity legible." On the other hand, we tried not to oversimplify. We have tried not to generalize the richness of the controversies to make our presentation worthy of interest (Venturini et al., 2015). To avoid this problem, we created a map parsimonious enough to be understandable and at the same time rich enough to show visually the multiple branches of the controversies at stake.

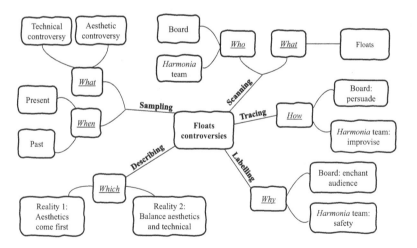

Figure 1 Visual representation of the controversy analysis.
Source: Elaborated by the authors.

Third moment

As our purpose is to write creatively, in the third moment of the analysis, we organize the data to tell a story of the carnival production. Rather than presenting only a cold map of controversies, we also sought to show that controversies are, in a certain way, similar to a movie in which characters experience drama, face conflicts, find resolutions. To do so, we draw on the paradigm of a screenplay elaborated by screenwriter Syd Field, in his 2005 book, *Screenplay: The Foundation of Screenwriting*. A screenplay can be defined as "a story told with pictures, in dialogue and description, and placed within the context of dramatic structure" (Field, 2005, p. 19–20).

According to Field (2005), the paradigm for a screenplay is divided into Acts I, II and III and two transitions points called plot points. Next, we describe each of the three Acts, using the paradigm of a screenplay and the notion of plot points, showing how we employed them in the data analysis. The map presented in Figure 1 was helpful to give us a broad perspective on the controversy, facilitating the creation of the story. To create the story, we organized the five focal points (sampling, scanning, tracing, labelling, and describing) into the three Acts of the paradigm of a screenplay. Since controversies are about conflict and "all drama is conflict" (Field, 2005, p. 25), the focal points suitably fit the dramatic action required in the three Acts, as we will show next.

Act I is the Set-up

Act I is the starting point in which the action unfolds in the dramatic context called the Set-up. In this unit of the screenplay, "the screenwriter sets up the story, establishes character, launches the dramatic premise (what the story is about), illustrates the situation (the circumstances surrounding the action), and creates the relationships between the main character and the other characters who inhabit the landscape of his or her world" (Field, 2005, p. 23, italics in the original).

Analysis procedure

We set up the story by gathering the data from sampling and scanning. *Scanning* allowed us to establish the characters: board, *harmonia* team and floats. Once we identified the characters in the floats controversy, we were able to create a relationship between them. As researchers enact the reality they are studying (Law, 2004), we added the researcher as part of the story. We use the data of the *sampling* stage to define the dramatic premise: Sasc was competing in the contest of the samba school but was doing so while having serious problems with the floats. Sampling was also helpful to illustrate the situation: the floats' problems arose many years ago, creating a conflict between the board and the *harmonia* team.

Act II is the Confrontation

Act II is the story's development, in which the dramatic action takes place in the context of confrontation. In this unit of the screenplay, "the main character encounters obstacle after obstacle that keeps him/her from achieving his/her dramatic need, which is defined as *what the character wants to win, gain, get, or achieve during the course of the screenplay* [...] All drama is conflict. Without conflict, you have no action" (Field, 2005, p. 25, italics in the original).

Analysis procedure

Labelling helped us identify the main characters' dramatic need: success in the samba school parade. By knowing why these actors were involved in the controversies, we established the story's conflicts. It was the different viewpoints about floats that led to technical problems in the artefactual objects they were using to create their float. *Tracing* was used to analyse the conflicts caused by the problems on parade day. These problems were put in the story as the obstacles that made it difficult for the main characters to achieve their dramatic need. Throughout the story, the search for conflict resolution during the parade generated action (e.g., improvised solution).

Act III is the Resolution

Act III is the closing of the narrative in which the action resolves the story in the dramatic context called Resolution. It is worth noting that Act III's resolution does not imply the end of the story. Field (2005, p. 26, italics in the original) highlights that "resolution does not mean ending; *resolution means solution* [...] the ending is that specific scene or shot or sequence that ends the script".

Analysis procedure

Controversies may be closed in different ways (Venturini, 2010a), and their closure is always open to debate. Thus, *describing* allowed us to analyse data so that we resolve the story without ending it: the samba school concluded the parade but conflicts over the floats remained open. As in some movies, room is left for the continuation of the dramatic action in a sequel to the movie.

Plot point

Plot points are transitions from one Act to another. A plot point is defined as *"any incident, episode, or event that hooks into the action and spins it around in another direction"* (Field, 2005, p. 26, italics in original).

Analysis procedure

To create the plot point, we select dramatic events identified in earlier moments of the analysis and use them to hook into the actions that would unfold in the next Acts. The two plots point can be viewed in Figure 2.

Based on the paradigm of a screenplay and its elements described earlier, we organized the map of controversies so that we could transform it into a story about a specific moment of the fieldwork. Figure 2 shows the story we created, using the paradigm of a screenplay as a frame.

Next, we present the story created after the data analysis process.

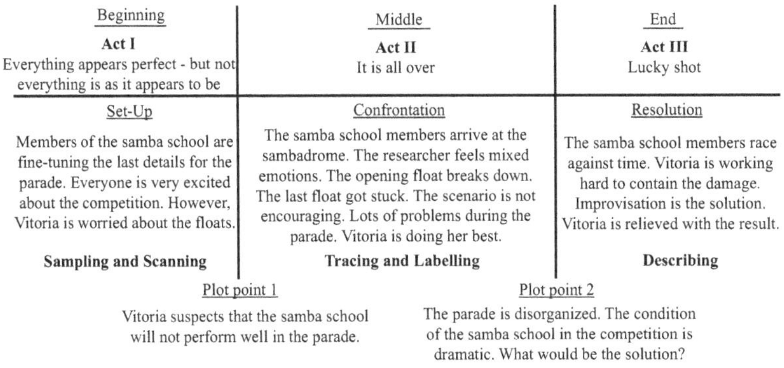

Beginning	Middle	End
Act I Everything appears perfect - but not everything is as it appears to be	**Act II** It is all over	**Act III** Lucky shot
Set-Up	Confrontation	Resolution
Members of the samba school are fine-tuning the last details for the parade. Everyone is very excited about the competition. However, Vitoria is worried about the floats.	The samba school members arrive at the sambadrome. The researcher feels mixed emotions. The opening float breaks down. The last float got stuck. The scenario is not encouraging. Lots of problems during the parade. Vitoria is doing her best.	The samba school members race against time. Vitoria is working hard to contain the damage. Improvisation is the solution. Vitoria is relieved with the result.
Sampling and Scanning	**Tracing and Labelling**	**Describing**

Plot point 1

Vitoria suspects that the samba school will not perform well in the parade.

Plot point 2

The parade is disorganized. The condition of the samba school in the competition is dramatic. What would be the solution?

Figure 2 The application of the paradigm of a screenplay.
Source: Adapted from Field (2005).

The story of the floats' controversies

Creative writing (Vickers, 2010; 2015) can capture the emotions and aesthetic aspects of everyday life (Gabriel & Özkazanç-Pan, 2013; Taylor, 2000). Different forms of creative writing provide "a useful addition to our ways of thinking about organizations and an indispensable approach to strengthening the connection between organizational analysis as an academic discipline and the subjective experience of organizational memberships" (Phillips, 1995, p. 625). Watson (2000) uses a specific type of creative writing: ethnographic fiction. Ethnographic fiction uses elements of a novel such as narratives, dialogues, scene description and author emotions. At the time, "the events, emotions and insights which are written about are all ones derived from observations and experiences gained by the writer as an ethnographic researcher" (Watson, 2000, p. 490). It is an approach that helps to create reader engagement, encouraging the readers to use their imagination to make sense of the organizing being depicted (Savage, Cornelissen & Franck, 2018). Creative writing can be a source of inspiration for experimenting with new ways of thinking and questioning the status of the organizing observed (Pick, 2017). These notions align with controversy analysis for two main reasons.

First, mapping controversies requires not only presenting a map of conflicts, disagreements and debates, it also concerns the creation of a narrative arc that helps readers make sense of the data. With Venturini, we believe that "a good scientific paper is not just a pile of facts: It is a good story in the same way a good crime novel is not just a game of clues" (Venturini et al., 2015, p. 83), an insight shared by Alvesson and Kärreman (2007, 2011). Second, controversy analysis is a powerful tool to investigate the (marginal) viewpoints that question taken-for-granted organizational practices and discourses (Venturini, 2010a,b). Joining a cartography of controversies with creative writing is a promising path for collecting and analysing qualitative data.

The story presented below is an ethnographic fiction. Nevertheless, it is also grounded, as it is based on specific fieldwork research conducted by the first author. The experience described involves the researcher interacting with the school members from the school's hall until the Sambadrome. The story we create is not intended to be exhaustive concerning all the controversies carried out in the research. Instead, we chose an episode of the fieldwork in which it was possible to show the implications of the controversies for organizing the samba school's parade. The description of the parade helps to present how it is possible to use fictional narratives to describe the results of research based on controversy analyses.

The samba school's name and its members have been withheld to keep identities confidential. The first author's main informant has been given the fictitious name Vitoria. Furthermore, this episode also illustrates the mixed and ambiguous emotions of the researcher during his fieldwork experience.

Act I: Everything appears perfect – but not everything is as it appears to be…

It was midnight. I had just arrived at Sasc hall (see Figure 3). This was the meeting point for all the samba school members. It was from there that several buses were heading to the Sambadrome. Vitoria stood in front of me. She was my informant and one of the most experienced coordinators of the *harmonia* team. Vitoria was 42 years old and had already played several roles in carnival production since she started working at the samba school long ago. She was smart, kind and passionate about the carnival and very strict with rules and safety. I learned a lot from her about what people can and cannot do during carnival production.

A few days earlier, she told me not to take my bag with my fieldwork material (camera, field notebook and pens) because I was forbidden to take pictures during the parade and might lose my material during the hubbub in the competition waiting area.[3] As a result, I had only my clothes (jeans, white sneakers and a white shirt) and my ID card, mobile phone and some pocket money. Next to Vitoria was her daughter, Teresa. She was 18 years old and started attending samba school activities when she was still a child. Different from her mother, she was tall as well as strong. Teresa was a member of the *alegoria* team that supports the float coordinators, creating the decorations and props that you see on the floats and in the costumes.

This photo was taken on a rehearsal day at the samba school hall. These events are used to rehearse the samba theme (singing and playing the drums) and provide fun and entertainment for the community. In these events, many controversies about the floats are debated between the *harmonia* team and the board.

Figure 3 Inside the samba school hall.
Source: First author files.

The street was packed with people, many carrying their costumes and others already partially costumed. As arranged a few weeks earlier with Anderson, one of the *harmonia* team members, I was supposed to dress as a *merendeiro*[4] and the costume would be handed to me just before the parade. The place was very busy with many cars, buses and people circulating through the nearby streets. I saw several members of the *harmonia* team walking up and down with sheets of paper and talking to other members of the Sasc. Some were shouting, others were gesticulating. They were arranging the last details before we left for the parade site. Considering that the parade is highly competitive, there is no room for error. Otherwise, the samba school would not end up as the parade's champion. The members of the Sasc are confident that they will conquer one more championship. Everything looks perfect but not everything is as it appears to be.

Although everyone was excited and confident, the expression on Vitoria's face was not good. She was apprehensive about something; she did not seem to be really paying attention to our conversation. Suddenly, she turned to me and said, "We are playing the odds. The floats are not ready to parade. We did not have enough time and money to get them ready."

Flashback

At this point, I began to remember several episodes in which controversies arose around the floats: the *harmonias* constantly complained about the school board's lack of attention to the technical aspects of the floats. They said that the board was only concerned with the aesthetics. Months ago, in a conversation with Mauro (the coordinator of the shed), he said that the floats were old, very heavy and full of patches. Weeks before the parade day, I visited the shed where the floats were built and realized that some of their parts still needed to be finished. On this day, Mauro uttered harsh criticisms of the board members.

My thoughts were interrupted by Vitoria completing her reasoning: "this is the recipe for failure. Our club runs the risk of being relegated to the second division of the competition." After six months of intense field-work, I was emotionally linked with the samba school members. I was also worried about the school's performance. Moreover, Anderson, the *harmonia* who was supposed to bring my costume, still had not shown up. It is forbidden to parade without a costume, making me anxious and raising doubts about whether I would be allowed to observe the parade. Two big problems, with the night just beginning. In front of us, a parked bus. It was time to leave for the Sambadrome.

Act II: It's all over now

Part 1: There is no costume

The bus parked near the Sambadrome (see Figure 4 for the inside view of the Sambadrome). We are in the competition waiting area (see Figure 5). Vitoria was told that her daughter, Teresa, would replace one of the float people who had not shown up. A few minutes later, Teresa walked through the floats towards me, in costume. She said, "Hello everyone!" and Vitoria led her to the float on which she would parade. Different from them, I still had no outfit to wear. Right after they left, to make matters worse, Anderson came over and said that there were no *merendeiro* outfits left. At that moment, I thought I would be unable to parade and became very frustrated. Anderson was in a hurry. He gave me this information and ran off to help the other members of the *harmonia* team.

Vitoria came back to the place where I was. I told her about what I had just heard from Anderson. She looked at me with an angry face and, putting both hands on her head, she said, "It's unbelievable! I had told Anderson to separate your costume into a different bag, so we wouldn't risk someone taking it. These guys just can't do their job right." Then, a new member of the *harmonia* team asked Vitoria for help with the float that was concerning her. She told me to wait in that place and that she would find a solution for my costume.

The photo, Figure 4, was taken on the day of a technical rehearsal at the Sambadrome. In the left part of the photo, further back, it is possible to see the entrance portal to the parade avenue. This photo is from the opposite angle to the next photo.

Figure 4 Parade Avenue. Inside the Sambadrome.
Source: First named author files.

The photo, Figure 5, was taken on the day of a technical rehearsal at the Sambadrome. In the upper part of the photo, it is possible to see the entrance portal of the parade avenue. The people

Figure 5 Competition waiting area.
Source: First named author files.

with number 80 on the back are members of the *harmonia* team. The other people are not from the *harmonia* team but are also members of Sasc.

The situation made me even more concerned. If I could not get a costume, I would not be allowed to join the parade down the avenue. The parade of samba schools was the climax of my fieldwork, something for which I had waited a long time. I knew that being there would be a rich data source for my research and a unique experience in understanding the closing of a one-year cycle of carnival production.

I was experiencing mixed feelings. On the one hand, I was filled with positive emotions of joy, feeling excited and full of curiosity. The Sambadrome is a magical place. It is a place where carnival dreams become a reality. Huge and beautiful floats, colourful costumes and lively music blend with the exciting singing from the spectators that adds a special touch to the show. Nevertheless, at the same time, I was also worried, anxious, tense and confused about what would happen in the next few minutes. I was wondering: "Will I parade? Will the floats be able to parade without problems?"

After solving problems with one of the floats, Vitoria returned to where I was standing, looking clearly hopeless and feeling dejected. Demonstrating optimism, she said, "Come on, don't worry about it. I had an idea. You can wear my daughter's *alegoria* costume. Remember, she's replacing a person on the float. You can play her role on the *alegoria* team." Smiling and making fun of me, she added, "Don't worry, it's a unisex costume! Anyway, it's carnival." She picked up Teresa's *alegoria* costume and told me to put it on. Luckily, Teresa was a tall and strong girl. So, although the suit was a little tight, it fitted me. Finally, I am ready to parade. Looking at me and making a thumbs-up sign, Vitoria said, "Not bad! You're definitely going on the parade!".

Part 2: Oh my God!

I had on my *alegoria* costume. The percussion section was warming up. All the segments of the samba school were in place, facing the avenue. Vitoria told me to place myself next to the opening float. The percussion section started to play the samba theme. I was close to Vitoria. We were waiting for the siren to start the parade. It was almost time to show the result of a year of hard work to the audience. The excitement of the Sasc members was contagious. Everyone was singing and seemed joyful. I had ambiguous feelings: anxiety, excitement, nervousness as well as joy. It was my first time in that magical place. The energy was intense, everything was so fantastic that sometimes I forgot that I was collecting data for my research and that the floats were in a desperate condition. One of the board members came up to us and said, "This year we will be the champion. I've never seen the school so beautiful and majestic." Vitoria responded optimistically, "We did our best. We deserve it." Vitoria and the board member walked away from me.

A few minutes later, I saw Vitoria talking with the other two members of the *harmonia* team. All of them looked concerned. One of the guys walked away and started looking in detail at the mechanical parts of the opening float. He came back and made a questioning face. Vitoria moved her head, clasped both hands together and put them in the air as if she asked for help. That was not a good sign. The opening float was the hardest to assemble, as it had three separate and heavy parts that had to be fitted together. The reaction of Vitoria reminds me of a conversation we had in the shed of the samba school.

Flashback

Researcher: Are the float's structures old?

Vitoria: They are very old. We use solder and hammers, as well as iron and wood pieces to fix them constantly. That is, we take a piece of iron that is somewhere out there and say: "Oh, let's solder it here," do you understand?

Researcher: But why not to build a new structure?

Vitoria: That is the question that will not go away. It demands investment. You have to take all the floats apart. The samba school board would have to talk with some people from the *harmonia* team. They would have to talk with Mauro, who would see the bearing and the seam in question, for example, do you understand? He would see what needs to be done. You need to remove some iron, there is too much. The gears do not work one hundred percent. The tyres are of different calibres. It is cheaper to use iron on iron. What happens at the end of the process? The float structure is already too heavy. Board members focus only on the aesthetic aspects of floats.

When the Sambadrome siren rang at about 6:45 a.m. and Sasc started to participate, the excitement built up, everyone started to sing the samba theme with even more passion. From the competition waiting area, I could see that the public was also very excited. The *merendeiros* were doing the pushing and the *harmonias* were making sure the pace was right.

Everything was going well until suddenly, the shaft connecting two parts of the opening float broke apart. There was a big commotion. It was an agitated moment. Vitoria began to cry. She said, "Oh my God, it is all over!" The Sasc's members and the *merendeiros* promptly tried to put the shaft back in place. One of the Sasc's directors came running up and asked, "What the hell is going on?" Vitoria glared at him but said nothing. It was challenging to connect the two parts because the floats weigh tons and moving them is not easy. After a lot of effort, shouting and swearing, all the parts were properly assembled. When that happened, there was general relief from Sasc members. Vitoria looked at me and gave the thumbs-up sign.

However, as everyone returned to their original positions in the parade, I heard a noise. There was a small explosion on the other side of the float. It was possible to hear many cries of despair. Fortunately, no one was hurt. A wire that provided energy to light the float sculpture got tangled up in its gear and generated a small explosion. The large amount of iron in the float made placing the wires on the float difficult. The *harmonia* team quickly put out the fire using old rags that were nearby. By that time, several minutes had passed. As the parade had already started, part of the segment ahead was already on the avenue. If the float could not approach the group in front of it, it would harm the Sasc, causing a loss of points. The championship title was at stake.

The fire was put out. Now, the float was ready to move again. The *harmonia* team desperately signalled and shouted for the float to be pushed as quickly as possible. To everyone's relief, the Sasc members were able to push the float close to the segment before it reached the yellow line[5] so the school entered the avenue without any gaps.[6] Vitoria returned to her position in the parade. At this point, the controversies that had occurred in previous years and during the production of the floats began to haunt the samba school nervously as they began the parade. For several minutes after this first incident, the parade ran normally. Overcoming this initial hurdle seemed to have provided more fuel for Sasc members. Everyone's energy and joy were contagious.

Half the time of the parade had passed when from afar I saw Vitoria and some other members of the *harmonia* team, running in the opposite direction of the parade. While they were screaming, I could not hear because of the noise of the music and the crowd singing. Vitoria came close to me and said, "please go back down the avenue and help the team in the waiting area. We just received a message on the walkie-talkie that the last float got stuck." They recruited as many people as possible to help with the last float without harming the rest of Sasc's parade. I was available. So, I rushed to help.

Flashback

As I headed for the waiting area, I remembered that the last float was a source of much conflict. A part of its gear was hastily built and was in danger of failing. Vitoria had communicated to the board about this problem. A week before the parade, I helped the *harmonia* team move the floats from the shed to the Sambadrome. It took several nights of pushing the heavy floats to get them to the waiting area. The last float was the most difficult to push because it already had a problem that made it difficult to move, as shown in Figure 6.

Figure 6 Pushing floats to waiting area.
Source: First author files.

Upon arriving at the waiting area, I saw several samba school members pushing the last float. I asked a Sasc director how I could help. He told me that the last float was very heavy and could not enter the avenue because of an incline in the waiting area. To make matters worse, part of the gear was misplaced, dragging across the floor, making it difficult for the float to move. I followed the director's instructions and positioned myself at the back of the float to push it. After a few minutes, we overcame the slope and moved the float. But it was already too late. When the float managed to enter the avenue to parade, the rest of the samba school was several metres away. This created a huge gap between the last float and the segment in front of it.

A big gap between the samba school segments is a serious fault that the *Julgadores*, the judges, would penalize. In addition to the title of champion seeming lost, the school also ran the risk of being relegated to the second division of the competition if its score was too low. I saw Vitoria talking to other members of the *harmonia* team. She looked very disappointed. She knew that Sasc's odds in the competition were dramatically shortening.

Act III: Lucky shot

A crisis management team was formed spontaneously. Vitoria, a member of the board and two members of the *harmonia* team, gathered on the side of the avenue. I observed everything closely, although I could not hear the conversation because of the noise of music, drumming and singing. They seemed to be talking about a possible solution to the gap problem. The director was gesticulating a lot and looking angry. Vitoria tried to calm him down as she gave instructions to the other two team members. Then, she came walking towards me. The other three team members headed the other way.

Vitoria told me: "we are going to improvise to try to minimize the penalty for our failure." The director of Sasc would gather a group of members of the samba school to parade in front of the float, filling the gap that created a large space. Considering the size of the gap, the problem would hardly be solved completely. The solution might eventually reduce the penalty imposed by the jurors.

The other solution was to reduce the speed of the parade so that the float could reach the other segments of the samba school. With that, Sasc would not parade all over the avenue with a big gap. Vitoria told me to go with her to the front of the parade. Along the way, she communicated by walkie-talkie with a Sasc's director. She wanted to make sure the samba school members knew that they should parade slower. The decrease in the parade speed made it possible to reduce the gap. However, some minutes later, this created another problem. Samba schools need to parade within a limited time. While the problems were resolved, the pace of the parade was impaired. The controversies in the production of the floats generated a ripple effect during the parade.

The *harmonia* team communicated desperately by walkie-talkie again to ask the last segments of Sasc to increase the speed of the parade. The samba school had to parade fast enough to reach the end of the avenue in time but not so fast as to disrupt the parade's pace and lose points due to disorganization. At that moment, I was already in the dispersion area[7] with Vitoria. She was coordinating the parade through the walkie-talkie. The clock was ticking down. There were only a few minutes left, with part of the school still parading down the avenue. If Sasc could not complete the parade on time, it would be penalized. Controversies over the production of the floats were haunting the samba school until the last minute of the parade.

We saw Teresa, daughter of Vitoria. She had just arrived at the dispersion area and joined us. Everyone was apprehensive and followed the countdown to the end of the parade time on the Sambadrome clock.

The last members of the school were still on the avenue. In the dispersion area, people sang the school's samba. However, it was still not possible to celebrate. The gates began to be closed.

Quickly, the remaining Sasc members crossed through the gates and arrived in the dispersion area. Total relief. Everyone hugged each other. There was much celebration. By very little, Sasc did not exceed the time limit. After that explosion of feelings, I approached Vitoria and asked her what she thought of the parade. Looking very tired, she replied: "Today we got a lucky shot."

It was 10 a.m. of the day after our night of carnival. We had just arrived at Sasc hall after the parade. The streets were empty. Many Sasc members left the Sambadrome to go straight to their homes. There's a lot of dirt on the floor, leftover costumes and unused material left behind. The *harmonia* team members who came to the hall, Vitoria included, were frustrated on the one hand but relieved on the other. Vitoria looked at me with a sense of mission accomplished, took a deep breath, and said: "Next month, the carnival production cycle starts all over again."[8]

Final considerations

This chapter presents a technique for collecting and analysing data and creative writing to show the research findings through ethnographic fiction. Based on a cartography of controversy, researchers can bring to life the most vivid aspects of social interactions: the conflicting dynamics of negotiating divergent interests while having the same objective. In this case, to be champions of a samba school parade competition. In addition, in analysing the data, keep in mind a story that will be told based on the creative narrative provides opportunities for presenting the data in an interesting way that allows the reader to make sense of the reality that the researcher is enacting.

Reflective issues

Reflexively, try to think about these questions that can help you to design your protocol for collecting data and data analysis framework:

- Is it clear to you what controversies are?
- Why should you embrace past, cold, underground controversies and be wary of boundless ones?
- What focal points should you keep in mind and why are they important for controversy analysis?
- How can you use the focal point to analyse the data?

- Thinking about the story, how would you move to the next stage of theorizing, by identifying themes for orientation to further data collection, using Gioia, Corley and Hamilton (2013)?
- Reading the story, what actor networks would you map from the actors and actants, paying attention to the socio-materiality evident in the account, using Latour (2005)?

Complementary readings

Table 11 offers reading suggestions related to controversy analysis.

Table 6 Complementary readings on controversy analysis

Related methodological themes	Comments	Reading suggestions
Introduction to controversies	Cartography of controversies was developed to investigate contemporary socio-technical debate. It is a recurrent topic in science and technology studies.	Latour (2005), Pinch (2015), Pinch and Leuenberger (2006), Venturini and Munk (2021a,b), Yaneva (2012)
Collecting data	There are various techniques for collecting data and multiple data source are needed.	Venturini and Munk (2021a), Yaneva (2012)
Analysing data	There are various techniques for analysing data, from simple coding techniques to sophisticated digital tools.	Venturini and Munk (2021a), Yaneva (2012)
Empirical examples	Controversy analysis can be employed for various phenomena.	Callon (1986), De Pryck (2021), Michaud (2014), Scott, Richards and Martin (1990), Yaneva (2012)
International research projects on digital methods	There are different initiatives using cartography of controversies to investigate social media and public debates on the internet worldwide.	https://wiki.digitalmethods.net; https://medialab.sciencespo.fr/en; http://climaps.eu/#!/home; https://enforccast.hypotheses.org

Source: Prepared by the authors.

Notes

1 Sambadrome is the place where the samba school parade occurs.
2 *Alegoria* is a subgroup within the *harmonia* team. In Portuguese, floats are called *alegorias*, hence the group's name. Its members support the *harmonia* coordinators by helping its members with their costumes, placing them on the right spots on top of the floats, giving out information about who will be on each float and coordinating the *merendeiros* (*merendeiro*: see note 9) during the parade.
3 Competition waiting area is a place at the Sambadrome where the school members and floats assemble before the parade, awaiting the time to go on the avenue.
4 *Merendeiros* are the individuals responsible for pushing the floats during the parade. They are usually recruited among people known by the members of the *harmonias*. They get paid about $5.00 for the job, plus a packed lunch before the parade – hence the name *merendeiro* (lunch box receiver).
5 The yellow line at the beginning of the avenue marks the spot where the parade begins and from where the jurors can start evaluating the samba school.
6 If the jurors spot a large gap between segments or between a float and a segment, the samba school loses points.
7 Large area at the end of the avenue where the segments disperse and the floats are parked, until all the components of the parade are complete.
8 Sasc took third place in the competition.

References

Alvesson, M. & Kärreman, D. (2007). Constructing mystery: Empirical matters in theory development. *Academy of Management Review*, 32(4), 1265–1281.

Alvesson, M. & Kärreman, D. (2011). *Qualitative research and theory development: Mystery as method*. Thousand Oaks, CA: Sage.

Callon, M. (1986). Some elements of a sociology of translation: Domestication of the scallops and the fishermen of St. Brieuc Bay. In Law, J. (Ed.). *Power, action, and belief: A new sociology of knowledge?* (pp. 196–223). London: Routledge & Kegan Paul.

Clegg, S. R. (2000). The rhythm of the saints: Cultural resistance, popular music and collectivist organization in Salvador, Bahia in Brazil. In Linstead, S. and Hopfl, H. (Eds). *The aesthetics of organization* (pp. 246–263). London: Sage.

De Pryck, K. (2021). Controversial practices: Tracing the proceduralization of the IPCC in time and space. *Global Policy*, 12, 80–89. https://doi.org/10.1111/1758-5899.12910

Field, S. (2005). *Screenplay: The foundations of screenwriting*. New York, NY: Bantam Dell.

Gabriel, Y. & Özkazanç-Pan, B. (2013). Untold stories of the field and beyond: Narrating the chaos. *Qualitative Research in Organizations and Management*, 8, 4–15.

Gioia, D. A., Corley, K. G. & Hamilton, A. L. (2013). Seeking qualitative rigor in inductive research: Notes on the Gioia methodology. *Organizational Research Methods*, 16(1), 15–31.

Goldwasser, M. J. (1975). *O palácio do samba*: *Estudo antropológico da escola de samba Estação Primeira de Mangueira*. Rio de Janeiro: Zahar Editores.

Hussenot, A. (2008). Between structuration and translation: An approach of ICT appropriation. *Journal of Organizational Change Management*, 21(3), 335–347.

Hussenot, A. (2014). Analyzing organization through disagreements: The concept of managerial controversy. *Journal of Organizational Change Management*, 27(3), 373–390.

Hussenot, A. & Missonier, S. (2010). A deeper understanding of evolution of the role of the object in organizational process: The concept of 'mediation object'. *Journal of Organizational Change Management*, 23(3), 269–286.

Jarzabkowski, P., Langley, A. & Nigam, A. (2021). Navigating the tensions of quality in qualitative research. *Strategic Organization*, 19(1), 70–80.

Júlio, A. C. & Tureta, C. (2018). Turning garbage into luxury: the materiality in practices of the carnival production. *Brazilian Business Review*, 15(5), 427–443.

Latour, B. (2005). *Reassembling the social*: *An introduction to actor-network-theory*. Oxford: Oxford University Press.

Law, J. (1994). *Organizing modernity*. Oxford: Blackwell.

Law, J. (2004) *After method: Mess in social science research*. London; New York, NY: Routledge.

Michaud, V. (2014). Mediating the paradoxes of organizational governance through numbers. *Organization Studies*, 35(1), 75–101.

Phillips, N. (1995). Telling organizational tales: On the role of narrative fiction in the study of organizations. *Organization Studies*, 16(4), 625–649.

Pick, D. (2017). Rethinking organization theory: The fold, the rhizome and the seam between organization and the literary. *Organization*, 24(6), 800–818.

Pinch, T. (2015). Scientific controversies. In *International encyclopedia of the social and behavioral sciences* (pp. 281–286). Oxford: Elsevier.

Pinch, T. & Leuenberger, C. (2006). Researching scientific controversies: The S&TS perspective. In Proceedings of EASTS Conference 'Science Controversy and Democracy', National Taiwan University, Taiwan, August 3–5.

Savage, P., Cornelissen, J. P. & Franck, H. (2018). Fiction and organization studies. *Organization Studies*, 39(7), 975–994.

Scott, P., Richards, E. & Martin, M. (1990). Captives of controversy: The myth of the neutral social researcher in contemporary scientific controversies. *Science, Technology, & Human Values*, 15(4), 474–494.

Taylor, S. S. (2000). Aesthetic knowledge in academia: Capitalist pigs at the academy of management. *Journal of Management Inquiry*, 9(3), 304–328.

Tureta, C. & Américo, B. L. (2020). Gambiarra as an emergent approach in the entanglement of the organizational aesthetic and technical controversies: The samba school parade case. *Brazilian Administration Review*, 17(3), 1–26.

Tureta, C., Américo, B. L. & Clegg, S. (2021a). Controversies as method for ANTi-history, *Revista de Administração de Empresas*, 61(1), 1–12.

Tureta, C., Américo, B. L. & Clegg, S. (2021b). Controversies as method for ANTi-history: An inquiry into public administration practices, *Organization*, 28(6), 1018–1035.

Venturini, T. (2010a). Diving in magma: How to explore controversies with actor-network theory. *Public Understanding of Science*, 19(3), 258–273.

Venturini, T. (2010b). Building on faults: How to represent controversies with digital methods. *Public Understanding of Science*, 21(7), 796–812.

Venturini, T., & Munk, A. K. (2021a). *Controversy mapping: A field guide*. Cambridge: Polity.

Venturini, T., Ricci, D., Mauri, M., Kimbell, L. & Meunier, A. (2015). Designing controversies and their publics, *Design Issues*, 31(3), 74–87.

Vickers, M. H. (2010). The creation of fiction to share other truths and different viewpoints: A creative journey and an interpretive process. *Qualitative Inquiry*, 16(7), 556–565.

Vickers, M. H. (2015). Stories, disability, and 'dirty' workers: Creative writing to go beyond too few words. *Journal of Management Inquiry*, 24(1), 82–89.

Watson, T. J. (2000). Ethnographic fiction science: making sense of managerial work and organizational research processes with Caroline and Terry. *Organization*, 7, 489–510.

Yaneva, A. (2012). *Mapping controversies in architecture*. Manchester: Ashgate Publishing Company.

4 Writing

Theorizing aesthetically on inclusion

Bruno Luiz Américo, Fagner Carniel and Stewart Clegg

Keywords: Theorizing aesthetically; Qualitative Research; Rigour and aesthetics in qualitative research; Disability Studies; Deaf.

Expected learning outcomes

At the end of the chapter, readers will be able to:

- Address the challenges of writing a qualitative research paper theorizing aesthetically about organizations and organizing
- Appreciate the differences and complementarities between intellectual and aesthetic theorizing
- Find in aesthetic theorizing a means of living and enacting stories that combine experience and theory that considers complex, paradoxical, sensitive, emotional and ambiguous realities
- Learn about aesthetic theorizing by reading a short story theorizing aesthetically *with* deaf people's experiences and impairments, enacting people with disabilities as the producers of knowledge.
- Pay attention to the writers' ethical position concerning subjects (who must not become a docile body in their hands) and readers (who must be able to engage with the text without being guided by interpretations conditioned by its structure).

Introduction

This chapter aims to address the challenges posed by and the value that can be created through theorizing aesthetically about organizations

DOI: 10.4324/9781003198161-5

and organizing. To do this, we produce an exercise in aesthetic theorizing that arises from experience in vocational education with deaf students, drawn from our disability research experience, our work experiences with disability, as well as examination of fieldwork notes on the management learning of deaf students and interview transcripts of employees working with them. Some of the people working with the students, organizing disabled people's education, also had disabilities. The exercise in aesthetic theorizing considers the experiences and judgements (ambiguities, emotions) of writers, subjects and readers, as layers present in any text understood as a joint production or social reality (Strathern, 1987; Tierney, 2003).

The story we have written about disability is creatively based on real people, a real situation and actual data, as well as real experience. However, it was written after meeting profoundly deaf people and after we had bracketed sociological narratives about deafness. We decided to live some of the challenges and controversies involved in inclusion practices from our work and research contexts, with these people. It helped that one of the authors has a significant hearing loss in one ear, as well as some experience in researching the field of disability in practice (Clegg & Kreiner, 2013). By looking at the processes that characterized the Disabled People's Organisations Denmark (DPOD), an umbrella organization for 34 Danish disability organizations, he had an appreciation of the experience of hearing loss both practically and intellectually. For the latter, he was involved in a project designing a headquarters that expressed the needs of the 34 different disabilities that would use the building. The architects of the building were obliged to adopt the disabilities of each of the associations that would be housed in the building. Thus, they were blindfolded, put in wheelchairs, has their hearing cancelled by earmuffs and so on. They were obliged to do so because the members of the DPOD wanted to be sure that there was a proper understanding of the users' needs and capabilities. In addition, since 2007, the two Brazilian authors have been involved in bilingual education in Brazil, acting as teachers, taking on the educational policies of inclusion (Américo, Carniel & Takarashi, 2014), deafness (Carniel, 2013) and sign language (Carniel, 2018) as privileged objects of investigation. In this journey, they witnessed closely some of the leading social, pedagogical and organizational effects that the recognition of Brazilian sign language and the construction of bilingual education systems have had on Brazilian deaf communities.

We are not people with profound disabilities. For this reason, we chose not to occupy this existential, political and epistemological place in our narratives. Rather than trying to personify any deaf experience, the stories we tell take the point of view of someone who, either as a teacher or as a researcher, approaches this social universe. In doing so, one can learn something from the deaf about the plural and contradictory meanings that inclusive organizational and interpersonal practices generate from the social and subjective experiences of the many people disabled by their particular bodily, sensory or cognitive condition (Goodley, 2001; Oliver, 1996; Hughes, 2007; Thomas, 2007).

We assume that the "the construction of stories amounts to theory building. Stories tell us something about the world, thus directly making valuable contributions to knowledge" (Hansen, Barry, Boje & Hatch, 2007, p. 113), albeit that the story is just the beginning of analysis. Hence, to consider both aesthetic experience and judgement (Strati, 2000; Warren, 2008) on the part of writers, readers and subjects in the research process is essential (Taylor, 2000): as Warren (2008, p. 561) suggests, the research process is an intersubjectively constructed aesthetic experience and judgment. Rhodes and Brown (2005) suggest that if narrative fiction employs pragmatism, reflexivity and ethics, one must consider the writer's methodological and authorial responsibility to the researched subject; writers can "shift from a distant objective perspective to both an empathic and self-revealing one", enacting an account bearing the hallmarks of a "greater authenticity and transparency" (Hansen et al., 2007, p. 123).

Narrative fiction can move "the reader toward direct participation in knowledge building" (Hansen et al., 2007, p. 113) by enabling readers to interpret and become enmeshed in the story. For Ng and Cock (2002), reflexivity produces a relationship between writer and subject in which the reader becomes as an integral part of the text. Any text cannot exist in its effects apart from its reading or circulation. Reading entails interpretation and sensemaking, even of stories that claim to be 'true'. Any text is an occasion for reading and interpretation.

A few researchers have taken extraordinary steps to allow the reader to experience "the subjectivity of aesthetic experience", while recognizing that, "with aesthetic theorizing we don't all come to the same point, nor is that a desired goal" (Taylor, 2000, p. 309). Taylor (2000) included a play at the end of an article, writing the script for the play, *Capitalist Pigs,* in relation to a context that intrigued him: "the idea of employees being used up and then cast aside" (p. 305); the pig farm he created allowed him "to use the expressionistic device of having the pigs talk about being slaughtered when their time on the pig farm was done" (305). Hence, he linked up with theatre, striving to make intellectual ideas sufficiently visceral that readers and audiences could get "the idea in their gut" (305). Likewise, Elm and Taylor (2010, p. 132) affirm that presentational and artistic form "allows, encourages, and forces everyone to make sense of it themselves".

Being an analytical activity,

> intellectual theorizing emphasizes some parts or aspects of our experience at the expense of others (Morgan, 1997). Aesthetic theorizing can give us a sense of the whole or gestalt that can be missing from intellectual theorizing but is very much a part of our experience of the world.
>
> (Taylor, 2000, p. 308)

Writing an ethnographic account as a short story can be a potential tool with which to begin theorizing.

Differentiating intellectual/aesthetic theory and theorizing

The present chapter focus on 'theorizing' instead of 'theory'. However, what is the difference between 'theorizing' and 'theory'?

Here are several ideas about theory. First, Cornelissen, Höllerer and Seidl (2021, p. 5) assume that theory is "an explanation for a set of relationships between constructs". For these authors (2021, p. 5), the definition of theory guides and limits theorizing since it forces discussion of "processes of theorizing and criteria for evaluation proper to such a definition". Sandberg and Alvesson (2021, p. 3) affirm that "only regarding explanatory knowledge as 'theory' tends to limit the ways we theorize". Taylor (2000) states that a theory does not necessarily need to be expressed in terms of constructs and relationships between constructs from an organizational aesthetics perspective. For Phillips (1995) and Taylor (2002), a theory explains how specific aspects of the world works.

In contrast, theorizing is a practice that provides different forms of understanding, such as explanation, interpretation or emancipation (Cornelissen et al., 2021). Hence, "different forms of theorizing, as practices, are tied into different knowledge interests" (2021, p. 6), borrowing a formulation from Habermas (1971). Taylor (2000) argues that theorizing can be articulated in terms of narrative fiction: "just as the surface of contact between theory and quantitative data and theory and qualitative data have proven fruitful, so too can the surface of contact between theoretical ideas and narrative fiction" (Phillips, 1995, p. 635). Perhaps the best-known exponent of theorizing was Alan Blum (1971, p. 318), who defines it as an impulse to "make problematic" by methodically doubting the apparent nature of a phenomenon through the contemplation of other intelligible possibilities.

We link up with aesthetic theorizing in contemplating other intelligible possibilities by recognizing that any sense that is made of a phenomenon is a co-production of researchers, readers and subjects. The reader can read a story interpreting it as they will. No authors, researchers or subjects whose situational experiences provided data can stipulate its understanding. Interpretations cannot be imposed authoritatively (Ng & Cock, 2002). However, by the same light, while there is an interpretative space, not anything goes as there are also limits to understanding. In research terms, these consist of the data; hence best practice is to include the raw data from which the narrative of theorizing is built (Clegg, 1975). Theorizing does not mean that the research subjects become docile bodies in the author's hand (Biehl-Missal, 2015) but that the story woven is spun out of the data that it reflects on and 'makes problematic'.

Notably, the short story that follows problematizes ableism and definitions of disability depending on social constructions of context and impairment that are to be found in the workplace. It draws attention to how, in a school organization that calls on deaf people to give meaning to their social experience through normative expectations of non-disability, a negative ontology is produced (Campbell, 2009; Shakespeare, 1999; 2006). We report some of the conflicts and contradictions implicit in the ways in which deaf people negotiate their differences in educational organizations (Campbell, 2009). The role that the deaf body plays in the daily life of a bilingual school for deaf people is examined by focusing on people with disabilities as knowledge producers (cf. Williams and Mavin, 2012). After all, paying attention to the existence and experiences of people with disabilities in organizational contexts may be a gesture that helps us to theorize about projects for the future that are more accessible and inclusive for all people

A class in two stages

The classroom was set up. Upholstered chairs were arranged in a semicircle in front of the projector, which was turned off. The key turns, the teacher opens the door. The first ones rush in with the light still off. Gradually, the tightly planned symmetry is broken by the tumultuous presence of the group. Finally, the projection screen is fixed in place and the equipment turned on. The focus, carefully regulated, projects the title "Representations of deafness in the workplace".

Few are interested. Then, the teacher waves his arms to get attention in front of the class. No return, he decides to use the switch. The light blinks incessantly on and off a few times and almost everyone starts to pay attention. The eyes start to focus on the teacher. "Good morning!" signs the teacher. After presenting the topic, he starts his problematization by asking: "In the workplace, are you considered to be deaf or disabled?" A solitary voice, 'disabled', clashes with the classes' articulations, causing some embarrassment.

The perplexity of colleagues makes the class start to demand a consensus on the issue. The teacher just watches while the discussion takes place. "Don't you speak sign language!? So, you are deaf, not handicapped!" argues one girl. "Disabled is someone who has a problem. Deaf is someone normal!" says another. "Of course, I am disabled. Look at my exemption card…" the boy retorts, pointing to the bus card hanging around his neck. "It does not matter; I got my job as an administrative assistant thanks to an existing quota for people with disabilities – what counts is how you see yourself," says another.

What a start to class! Even an inexperienced teacher would have been delighted with the opportunity to articulate this discussion with the different identity representations that today dispute space and legitimacy in the daily lives of deaf people. However, more than a pretext to start a class, the question about the identity of these students evokes a problem that does not find a single and definitive solution: what is deafness, after all?

The second half of 2005 was drawing to a close; all the semester planning was behind him. It was already Friday, almost ten in the morning. The 50 minutes of that class flew by, full of dissent and controversies. All expressed opinions about how deafness was narrated in the workplace and surrounding society. "Deaf culture", "hearing impairment", "linguistic minority", "visual experience", "phonics", "difference" and "disability" were all discussed. It would be surprising not to get lost among language games with such complex signifiers!

Whenever possible, he wrote on the whiteboard the terms that were raised. Then, after creating a confusing web of terms, he used his 'Ariadne pen' to mark up and relate terms to guide the students quickly through the maze of terms and expressions created. Thus, saving time, he related two distinct discursive fields. On the one hand, work roles and identities are forged from the primacy of voice and oral language.

On the other, there is deafness and its linguistic and cultural expressions narrated either by the voice and gaze of others or by you, telling your story. That was the lesson. The class seemed to have grasped the difference between autonomy and submission, between being and not being. Its outcome, however, escaped the edges of the binary reasoning used by the teacher.

The last slide concluded: "Deafness is a social, cultural and linguistic manifestation of a marginalized social category in the workplace." Historically, these subjects have always occupied the peripheral place of 'others' in the socio-material discourse of hearing because of their absence of this capacity. Represented as 'strange', 'defective' or simply 'disabled', their ways of accessing the workplace differ because they do not listen; they cannot listen. Therefore, the teacher imagined that only the identity construction of deafness could offer an entire and independent existence for his students, current and future workers. However, a single disquiet pierced and disturbed the lesson: "Professor, does this mean that we are doomed to our deafness? So, what good is it for me to be deaf instead of disabled if I always perceive myself in relation to listeners?"

The buzzer rings: hearing it, the teacher signs to the class that is dismissed. The class hastily rises to go to the playground. Not knowing what to say, the teacher talks with the researchers who have been observing the scene, arguing that recognizing themselves as deaf would be a way of affirming their difference and showing their listeners that they are not the same. However, the girl who affirmed disability was right. She was right, in as much as countless socio-material discourses thematizing deafness in the workplace over the last century could only classify deaf people externally, placing them in front of the gaze (and hearing) of those that were not them, without ever revealing what they are. The girl brought up an ethical, political, social and epistemological issue for which the teacher was not prepared – and perhaps still is not.

More and more social thought has indeed shifted the issue of "identity problems" to the perception of "identities as a problem" themselves – Carlos Skliar pointed this out in his (unlikely) *Pedagogy of Difference* when denouncing the construction that is, at the same time, including and excluding the 'Other' in Western educational discourse. While the professor had studied this literature, he did not know how to translate this complex statement for his class. He gathered his stuff and walked to the door, thinking about it, without any conclusion. Nonetheless, it was the kind of problem he liked to take home.

On the way home, he recalled first meeting his wife, when they were very young, in a Baptist community on the west side of São Paulo. They studied at the same school, shared pedagogy at the same university and married a few months after graduation. When he got his first classes at a state college for deaf people across town, she soon started working there too. It was the early 1990s and he remembers how they immersed themselves in the universe of deafness. They lived in a time in which the political atmosphere was one of intense social mobilizations after the fall of the military dictatorship and they had firm hopes of rebuilding public institutions and democracy after decades of authoritarianism. They were listeners to conversations that seemed so freewheeling, filling the void that repression and censorship had created. They became involved, each in their way, in school and community life, with the desire to build a fairer world through education. They learned sign language, got to know students and their families, created groups to study the social history of deafness, organized activities around the clock, participated in political parties, met with local leaders, planned strategies to spread the agendas of the national movement of deaf people and agitated for bilingual education.

Everything went so fast. He had stayed at the school while she went back to university. She gained a master's degree, then a PhD, wrote books and has not stopped giving lectures. Gradually they had grown apart. There was not a fight nor an exact reason. Nothing the teacher could point out. The relationship had lost its spark, much as an open soda bottle loses its fizz over time. Nevertheless, of course, they still had their moments. Like that time in Brasília, after a week camped on the Esplanade of Ministries, awaiting the outcome of the vote on the Libras law in the National Congress – 2003 certainly left them very happy, as it represented a historic milestone in the process of recognition of sign language and deaf people in Brazil. However, it was a pity that moments of joy were getting rarer and rarer.

With all these memories crowding his mind on the way home, he thought that he would seek his wife's opinion on the day's happenings in the school. Between mouthfuls of Saturday lunch, the teacher decided to introduce the subject: "I know it is difficult for students to understand the history of the movement, they are young, they did not live that time, but I would like to do something to make them see the political importance of deafness; it is not just a word, it represents a long struggle for rights." After a moment of awkward silence, she raised her head and said calmly but firmly:

I understand that you want the best for them ... by erasing all the political construction that has been built around deafness, we would run the risk of eliminating language that exposes inequalities;

however, you can also consider that they are from another generation, that they understand themselves in a different way than people from our time and see the body and the language in other ways – even recognizing the struggles of the past, they will have to build their history looking to the future.

Probably, it was because of the puzzled expression of lack of agreement on the teacher's face that made her conclude with a slightly harsher tone: "I do not know, maybe you should just let them tell you how they are noticing and relating to all this visibility around deafness without wanting to frame their experience in an explanation that ... belongs in the 90s!". The teacher loved the spirit of Paulo Freire that flowed through his wife's reflections on the role of the school in the education of deaf people. However, at the same time, he hated her detachment from the history they had built together – "after all, why does she not appreciate our past!?"

No doubt it was an exaggeration. However, he did not understand it as such at the time. Besides, it is always challenging to teach a teacher who does not have much to teach about life. It is like teaching doctors that illness is just another way of living or, alternatively, explaining to husbands that their wives are not just wives, nor are they possessions in the way that 'their' suggests. It takes a long time to learn something that can help keep the world from falling apart. When you occupy these institutional places, of teaching, marriage, you must unlearn 24 hours a day!

With our teacher, it was no different, but it took time. It took more than ten years before he could return to the class to build other meanings out of it. Along the way, he lost money in the crisis of 2008, dropped out of school, separated from his wife, moved to another city, did a postgraduate degree in educational management and started a new profession, caught severe flu in 2010, remarried, had children and grew old, along with his generation's dreams. Brazil, which had taken off on the covers of magazines like *The Economist* as part of the BRICs, lost its way. First, it was routed at the 2014 FIFA World Cup to a disciplined German team, then returned to barbarism again in the 2018 elections – this time not even under the authority of the military but through the popular will expressed in the ballot box.

Despite being retired, as life flew past on the television, he decided to return to teaching and face classes again. In part, he felt that something needed to be done after the first lady's sign-language speech during Bolsonaro's inauguration — the president who, since re-democratization, was most clearly linked to the far right and the country's hate speech.

However, it was challenging to be restarting teaching while ceasing to be the teacher that he was. Time had passed not only for him but also for deaf schooling. The school was no longer the one he remembered.

Times had changed in Brazilian education. The shadow of neo-liberalism seemed to overshadow the republican project of a truly inclusive, democratic and citizen education that he had hoped for, for so long. Now that market logic was generalized in schools, the teacher experienced the pressure of offering his classes as a commodity among many others in the already disputed symbolic economy of educational 'quality'. His commodity status became more worn and less attractive with each ageing day.

Luckily, his job as a business administrator for the last decade, along with his postgraduate degree and experience in teaching deaf students, allowed him to teach vocational courses to four groups of hearing people and one of the deaf in the New Professional High School, a bilingual state school, right in the centre of the city of Diadema. Yes, that was no longer a school only for deaf people, like those he had known during the old network of special schools. Since 2006, the traditional special schools, which operated separately from regular Brazilian education, gradually became part of the common inclusive education network. The curricular architecture of professional education resolutely oriented to training individuals rather than producing more cultivated citizens was very modern. "But who would care about citizens when you can train entrepreneurial individuals?" – that was the ironic provocation he used to make to colleagues whenever he could.

The opportunity came at the very end of the first term when the Portuguese language teacher had to leave, with the teacher being assigned to two groups from different years of the Professional High School. The teacher entered the school's deaf classroom without much planning, with about three dozen hearing students behind him. There were already 17 deaf students in the room and the sign-language interpreter. The room was packed, some had to sit on the floor. He stood in the corner of the room, watching the crowd of deaf and hearing students mixed up, when Pedro, the class interpreter, asked him about the class.

Without any ceremony, the teacher just smiled and declared: "Well, let us take this opportunity and talk about inclusion!" He walked between desks and people, steering Pedro gently by the arm until they found a place where everyone could see them – "Guys, thanks for having us! At last, we will have a moment of integration. How about we take the opportunity to turn it into a truly inclusive class?" Then, while attention began to focus on them, he suggested:

I have a proposal for today, and it is straightforward. We talked in 1st B about the legislation that regulates inclusion policies in the labour market, but we do not know anything about the practical experience of deaf people in the workplace. As I know that some of the 4th A have already started their mandatory internships, I thought we could learn from your experiences; what do you think?

Embarrassed, Natalia asked: "Do you want us to explain to the listeners what it is like to be a deaf person in the workplace, teacher? But what do we learn from this?" "Yes and no", replied the teacher,

I think each one of you has something to say about the experience of being a deaf person for those who are not deaf. On the other hand, I also think that your experiences with deafness are different from each other and that we can all learn a little more about the situation of deaf people in Brazil if we pay attention to each other. What do you think?"

Before the class could sketch any reaction, he continued: "For example, Samantha, you have already done internships, and now you are at the City Hall, is it not correct? Could you please share this experience with us?"

Samantha was a lovely, energetic girl. Black, with thick, curly ethereal hair. She came from a middle-class family; her parents were teachers, and her older sister studied engineering in Belo Horizonte. They learned of her congenital deafness while she was in her mother's womb and, as soon as they could, mobilized all the resources they had to develop literacy in sign language; however, the support Samantha receives from her family is an exception in a world full of important issues affecting people with disabilities. Social isolation, discrimination, unemployment and a scarcity of resources are caused not by the disability itself but by people's attitudes, expectations and the environment as a whole. So, as her classmates like to say, Samantha gives the impression that she could "talk even under water". Now, she was an intern at the City Hall and was able to talk very enthusiastically about her experiences. She was a great student and got along well with the entire school, especially after participating in the 2016 student occupations when she was still in her 1st year. Knowing that, the teacher knew he could count on her to start the class.

Samantha spent about 15 minutes signing in front of the two groups with their mouths open. She explained in detail her work routine at the municipality's Finance Department. She narrated her arrival and praised the inclusive posture of the administrative technician who received her as an intern. According to her, Maria was not fluent in sign language but was trying to learn and prepare her department to expand the inclusion policies for people with disabilities. She detailed how Maria taught her to organize documents, issue notes, classify and enter accounting data. She reported the absence of other deaf people in any other positions and vehemently complained about the lack of awareness campaigns and sign language courses so that other colleagues could also better welcome her. At the end of her speech, she left a provocation in the air: "The challenge at any stage is always adaptation, but are we just the ones who need to adapt? Don't the institutions need to prepare to receive us?"

At that moment, questions and comments of all kinds rained down on her. Jessica, from 1st B, was curious to know: "Did you have to study maths to get the internship?" "Is it easier to work in the public sector than in the private one?" asked Cláudio, from the 4th grade. "Do you have access to the civil servants' salary? Tell us how much the teacher earns!" joked Jonathan, from 1st B. "Find an internship like this for me!" said her friend Ana, from 4th B. The question that most moved Samantha, however, came from Gerson, a thin, blond boy from 1st B whom the teacher did not know very well, who he presumed to be shy and relatively distant from the rest of his classmates: "I imagine you suffered much prejudice for being deaf. What do you do when this happens?"

Those seconds of silence that separated Gerson's question from Pedro's translation into sign language left the teacher a little worried. However, Samantha surprised him once again:

> It is true, it happens a lot that some people complain that the deaf here will take a while or will not even be able to do the job. However, the problem is not just that I am deaf. I am also a black woman. And then many people do not respect you because of that as well. Alternatively, they leave you there in a corner, not to do anything. That is why I always try to anticipate and know what needs to be done.

With indignation, and a certain amount of ingenuity, Ingrid from 1st B declared: "This is absurd! I cannot believe these things still happen!"

This was the cue for the teacher to take up the floor again and tell a little of what he knew about the history of the movement of deaf people in Brazil. He began by drawing attention to the fact that

Samantha's speech is critical, as it reminds us that we live in a very unequal and unfair world. Therefore, each generation needs to fight for its rights and build its citizenship based on the real problems and controversies it faces.

He then recalled the mobilizations from the 1980s to the 2000s, culminating in recognizing Brazilian Sign Language in 2003 and the regulation of bilingual education in 2005.

At the end of his brief historical recovery of the social struggles that preceded his deaf and hearing students' schooling, the teacher rehearsed a reflective synthesis:

The problem is that all these achievements of the 1st and 2nd generation of activism in the field of deafness do not solve the problems that many of you are facing nowadays, do they? You need, together, to establish new connections that can allow structural elements and actors to act, responding not only to those that have been causing the exclusion of different people throughout history but also offering a response to the consequences generated by such exclusive practices.

With the class still attentive, he concluded his participation:

That is why I consider Samantha's speech to be so significant. I think what she is showing us is that we are not just this or that. Each of us is made up of different identities that are interrelated. Unfortunately, the intersection of these identities leaves most people vulnerable to different forms of prejudice.

At that moment, the buzzer sounded, indicating the end of the class. As everyone stood up, Jessica and Gerson came over and said to the professor, in a low voice and synchronized manner: "How interesting what Samantha told us today. We should try to do something so that other people can also know stories like this. Then, perhaps, inclusion would no longer be seen as something that concerns only the disabled, right?"

Final considerations

Our objective was to discuss the challenges of writing a qualitative research paper that theorizes aesthetically about inclusive disability organizations and organizing, in which we must present the findings in ways that work for the writer (authors), readers (students, academics, researchers, professionals, editors, reviewers) and subjects (research interlocutors). We used the literary genre of the short story and the tools of fictional writing to theorize aesthetically about vocational education with deaf students from our disability research experience, our work experiences with disability, examination of fieldwork notes of management learning of deaf students and interview transcripts of workers with and without disabilities that are organizing disabled people's education. Hence, we hope that readers could live and enact complex, paradoxical, sensitive, emotional and ambiguous realities and situations, considering the lives of disabled people's experiences and judgements. Thus, our story problematized ableism and definitions of disability in the workplace due to social context and impairment.

Questions

1   Readers, do you believe that the aesthetic theorization presented in the form of a short story could create an understanding of issues related to disability today? What are they, in your analysis?
2   How do you experience and, above all, judge the short story you just read as an example of 'making something problematic'?

Reflective issues

Reflexively, try to answer these questions before starting to write and discuss your qualitative research data in the form of narrative fiction – or creative writing, autoethnography, poems, narrative semi-fiction – to theorize aesthetically:

*   Thinking of this short story, about the career of a teacher of deaf students and the changing social constructions of deafness as a disability, what important theoretical concepts can you extract from the narrative that could be developed analytically in further research?
*   What about your own research? Have you written an initial narrative about your data, whether in the form of categorization of data or narrative fiction?
*   How do your 'initial categories' or 'stories' relate to the specialized literature?
*   Do your 'tentative categories' or 'stories' make it possible to question or elaborate on the specialized literature?

- Does the constant reanalysis and rewriting of the data collected and analysed suggest the possibility of 'stabilizing categories' or a 'plot' from which to create and integrate a theoretical framework?

Finally, a table indicates complementary reading with methodological themes related to writing qualitative research that this chapter did not address in-depth.

Complementary readings

Please find reading suggestions below to deepen your knowledge about writing qualitative research and aesthetic theorizing.

Table 7 Complementary readings on writing

Related methodological themes	Comments	Reading suggestions
Introduction to research	Methodological books dealing with the basis and writing of qualitative research.	Flick (2008), Holliday (2007)
Writing plan or template	Thinking about qualitative research through a writing plan is a useful methodological practice.	Cassel, Cunliffe & Grandy (2017), Myers (2018)
Methodological concepts	Literary genres – tragedy, soap opera, a detective story – are methodological tools for qualitative research.	Ducrot and Todorov (1979), Rhodes (2002), Alvesson and Kärreman (2007), Alvesson and Kärreman (2011)
Organizational aesthetics	This field includes research on fiction and visual methods in Management.	Strati (2000; 2009), Gagliardi (2006). Taylor (2002), Warren (2002, 2008)

Source: Prepared by the authors.

References

Alvesson, M. & Kärreman, D. (2007). Constructing mystery: Empirical matters in theory development. *Academy of Management Review*, 32(4), 1265–1281.

Alvesson, M. & Kärreman, D. (2011). *Qualitative research and theory development: Mystery as method.* Thousand Oaks, CA: Sage.

Américo, B. L., Carniel, F. & Takahashi, A. R. W. (2014). Gestão pública da educação especial e formalismo nas políticas públicas inclusivas – o caso do Brasil. *Ensaio: Avaliação e Políticas Públicas em Educação*, 22(83), 379–410.

Biehl-Missal, B. (2015). 'I write like a painter': Feminine creation with arts-based methods in organizational research. *Gender, Work & Organization,* 22(2), 179–196.

Blum, A. F. (1971). Theorizing. In Douglas, J. D. (Ed.) *Understanding everyday life: Towards the reconstruction of sociological knowledge.* London: Routledge & Keagan Paul.

Campbell, F. K. (2009). *Contours of ableism. The production of disability and abledness.* Basingstoke: Palgrave Macmillan.

Carniel, F. (2013). A invenção (pedagógica) da surdez: sobre a gestão estatal da educação especial na primeira década do século XXI. 2013. Tese (Doutorado em Sociologia Política) – Universidade Federal de Santa Catarina, Florianópolis.

Carniel, F. (2018). A reviravolta discursiva da Libras na educação superior. *Revista Brasileira de Educação [online],* 23, e230027.

Cassell, C., Cunliffe, A. L. and Grandy, G. (2017). *The SAGE handbook of qualitative business and management research methods.* London: Sage.

Clegg, S. R. (1975) *Power, rule and domination: A critical and empirical understanding of power in sociological theory and organizational life.* London: Routledge and Kegan Paul.

Clegg, S. R. & Kreiner, K. (2013) Power and politics in construction projects. In Drouin, N., Müller, R. & Sankaran, S. (Eds.) *Novel approaches to organizational project management research: Translational and transformational* (pp. 268–293).Copenhagen: Copenhagen Business School Press.

Cornelissen, J., Höllerer, M. A. & Seidl, D. (2021). What theory is and can be: Forms of theorizing in organizational scholarship. *Organization Theory,* 2(3), p. 1–19.

Ducrot, O. & Todorov, T. (1979). *Encyclopedic dictionary of the sciences of language* (C. Porter, Trans.). Baltimore, MD: The Johns Hopkins University Press (*Dictionnaire encyclopedie des sciences du langage,* Paris 1973).

Elm, D. R. & Taylor, S. S. (2010). Representing wholeness: Learning via theatrical productions. *Journal of Management Inquiry,* 19(2), 127–136.

Flick, U. (2008). *Managing quality in qualitative research.* London: Sage.

Gagliardi, P. (2006). Exploring the aesthetic side of organizational life. In Clegg, S., Hardy, C. & Nord, W. (Eds). *Handbook of organizational studies* (pp. 701–724). London: Sage.

Goodley, D. (2001). 'Learning difficulties', the social model of disability and impairment: challenging epistemologies. *Disability & Society,* 16, 207–231.

Habermas, J. (1971) *Knowledge and human interests.* London: Heinemann.

Hansen, H., Barry, D., Boje, D. M. & Hatch, M. J. (2007). Truth or consequences: An improvised collective story construction. *Journal of Management Inquiry,* 16(2), 112–126.

Holliday, A. (2007). *Doing & writing qualitative research.* London: Sage.

Hughes, B. (2007). Being disabled: Towards a critical social ontology for disability studies. *Disability & Society,* 22, 673–684.

Myers, M. D. (2018). Writing for different audiences. In *The Sage handbook of qualitative business and management research methods* (pp. 532–545). London: Sage.

Ng, W. & Cock, C. D. (2002). Battle in the boardroom: A discursive perspective. *Journal of Management Studies*, 39(1), 23–49.

Oliver, M. (1996). *Understanding disability: From theory to practice*. Basingstoke: Macmillan.

Phillips, N. (1995). Telling organizational tales: On the role of narrative fiction in the study of organizations. *Organization Studies*, 16(4), 625–649.

Rhodes, C. H. (2002). Text. Plurality and organisational knowledge/I like to write about organisations. *Ephemera*, 2(2), 98–118.

Rhodes, C. H. & Brown, A. D. (2005). Writing responsibly: Narrative fiction and organization studies. *Organization*, 12(4), 467–491.

Sandberg, J. & Alvesson, M. (2021). Meanings of theory: Clarifying theory through typification. *Journal of Management Studies*, 58(2), 487–516.

Shakespeare, T. (1999). 'Losing the plot'? Medical and activist discourses of contemporary genetics and disability. *Sociology of Health & Illness*, 21(1), 669–688.

Shakespeare, T. (2006). *Disability rights and wrongs*. New York, NY: Routledge.

Strathern, M. (1987). Out of Context. *Current Anthropology*, 28(3), 251–281.

Strati, A. (2000). The aesthetic approach in organization studies. *Aesthetics of Organization*, 13, 34.

Strati, A. (2009). 'Do you do beautiful things?'. Aesthetics and art in qualitative methods of organization studies.' In Buchanan, D. & Bryman, A. (Eds). *The Sage handbook of organizational research methods* (pp. 230–45). London: Sage.

Taylor, S. S. (2000). Aesthetic knowledge in academia: Capitalist pigs at the academy of management. *Journal of Management Inquiry*, 9(3), 304–328.

Taylor, S. S. (2002). Overcoming aesthetic muteness: Researching organizational members' aesthetic experience. *Human Relations*, 55(7), 821–840.

Thomas, C. (2007). *Sociologies of disability and illness. Contested ideas in disability studies and medical sociology*. Basingstoke: Palgrave Macmillan.

Tierney, W. G. (2003). Undaunted courage: Life history and the postmodern challenge. In Denzin, N. & Lincoln, Y. S. (Eds). *Strategies of qualitative inquiry* (pp. 537–554). Thousand Oaks, CA: Sage.

Warren, S. (2002). Show me how it feels to work here: using photography to research organizational aesthetics. *Ephemera*, 2(3), 224–245.

Warren, S. (2008). Empirical challenges in organizational aesthetics research: Towards a sensual methodology. *Organization Studies*, 29(4), 559–580.

Williams, J. & Mavin, S. (2012). Disability as constructed difference: A literature review and research agenda for management and organization studies. *International Journal of Management Reviews*, 14, 159–179.

Conclusion

Imagination and creativity in qualitative research

César Tureta, Bruno Luiz Américo and
Stewart Clegg

Introduction

Drawing on different styles of creative writing, the book provides a distinctive approach to enacting qualitative research. Central issues for conducting qualitative research that are addressed included negotiating access, reviewing the literature, collecting/analysing data, theorizing and writing up research creatively. Using a storytelling approach, readers were presented with approaches for understanding texts, concepts, techniques and protocols. Each chapter brought an innovative perspective on one qualitative research process topic.

Although we offered specific examples of phenomena and organizations throughout the book to illustrate our explanation in each chapter, the approach presented can be used in other contexts. When reading this book, researchers should relate its ideas and challenges to their research design and the conditions faced in fieldwork. Researching through qualitative research methods requires flexibility in the continuous back and forth between research design, data collection and analysis, writing and theorizing. We recognize and assume this condition to be a strength and not a weakness of qualitative research. Readers can use the book as a guide for developing their research, doing so imaginatively and creatively rather than as suggestions and recommendations that should be followed as a blueprint for doing research. As we have stressed, research is a process of creative and imaginative enactment in which every researcher should be empowered to be their own methodologist, echoing Mills' (2000) note on 'intellectual craftsmanship' in his book, *The Sociological Imagination*. Empowerment comes from building capability in approaches; creativity and imagination come from the application of this capability to unique research contexts and questions.

DOI: 10.4324/9781003198161-6

The approach presented in this book is neither superior nor more valuable than other qualitative research methods, of which there are many. By the same token, we are not arguing that scholarship should abandon traditional scientific methods entirely in favour of storytelling approaches. Using different methods and approaches, all of which have something to offer, multiplies understanding of the realities created. Just as we used our imagination, creativity and experience to develop a book designed to be both useful and easy to understand, we trust that readers will also explore their creative potential to engage in qualitative research. The need to 'make problematic' aspects of contemporary life, demands no less. After all, "creativity and imagination can serve as worthy inputs to credible, scholarly research" (Vickers, 2013, p. 146).

Facing challenges in enacting qualitative research

When producing the book, one of our aims was to offer tools, paths and recommendations for researchers in designing and enacting qualitative research to deal with the challenges, problems and uncertainties of fieldwork and the interpretation of the data produced. Based on our experience as qualitative researchers, inductive research is well suited for the task. According to Eisenhardt, Graebner and Sonenshein (2016), inductive research is suited to handling situations in which it is difficult to find clear answers to the puzzles uncovered by researchers. Especially, this will be the case when dealing with grand challenges, such as creating more sustainability, ensuring the well-being of citizens and developing secure and resilient societies. Research that engages with these big issues requires flexible inductive methods (Eisenhardt et al., 2016).

Qualitative scholars face distinct challenges when they conduct research. Bansal and Corley (2012, p. 512) highlight that

> qualitative researchers often do not even know the theory they will anchor their insights on prior to collecting the data. Where they land may be very different from where they started. This iterative process poses immense challenges to qualitative researchers.

These challenges are not going to be resolved by a recipe book approach to methods which prescribes the exact ingredients, the processes for their combination and the precise sequencing to be used. Challenges of fieldwork and doing qualitative research require, as Mills (2000) argues, sociological imagination and creative thinking, generating novel ideas in encountering and enacting the field. Qualitative research encourages you to explore. Explore theories, explore data, explore the range of your imaginative responses to both theories and data. As Eisenhardt, Graebner and Sonenshein (2016) summarize, the relevance of creativity and generation of novel ideas in qualitative research entails:

> Creating novel ideas that can contribute to solving and explaining grand challenges is well suited to inductive methods [...] inductive research usually begins with a research question but without prede-fined constructs and theoretical relationships. This lack of a priori theory may lead to novel ideas for two reasons. First, the research is likely to explore unusual settings and unexpected perspectives – precisely the situations in which novel ideas probably exist – rather than examine familiar situations in which plausible hypotheses can be generated [...] Second, inductive research is likely to uncover those novel ideas because it is unconstrained by prior hypotheses and the need for quantitative data. Inductive research combines openness and discipline in other ways that privilege novel ideas. It relies on the discipline of data collection protocols and sample designs, but these may change as new insights and opportunities emerge. Furthermore, it relies on an analytic process, grounded theory building, that is open to novel ideas yet disciplined by data. Moreover, this discipline is central to the creativity and surprise that is so often associated with inductive methods
>
> (p. 1115)

For Bansal and Corley (2012), the richness of qualitative research cannot be reduced to a few tables that show data in seemingly objective numbers. A key task of qualitative researchers is to create novel ideas that present findings capable of helping readers to appreciate the field-work context. Doing this provides readers with unique and rich insights into experiences observed. Researchers should embrace the process of *doing* research rather than obsessing too much about planning it in advance. Experiencing life is easily missed when you are busy making other plans. Qualitative research requires *lived experience*. Qualitative studies explore ideas rather than faithfully following a plan set at the beginning of the research design (Bansal & Corley, 2012). Of course, this is an approach that can sometimes cause ethics committees, with their bias towards natural science methods being mapped out in advance, some concerns. These are best met by indicative planning that stresses that things can change and that major changes will be communicated. Indicative planning appreciates that the research life lived in experien-cing others and their situations may well creatively qualify even the best anticipations. The point is, qualitative researchers must nurture openness to experience, making them more flexible in conducting research.

Lessons and tips

- Global crises such as pandemics and climate change pose grand challenges for researchers as these issues redefine the experience of everyday life. Such events spur new forms of engagement with research, leading to scholars rethinking their scientific methods in the immediacy of their experience encountering data that challenges, as well as response to them, create.
- Qualitative research allows for flexibility when collecting and analysing data regarding novel experiences such as responses to a pandemic, climate catastrophes or other experiences that deeply unsettle everyday life.
- To investigate unknown phenomena, researchers must embrace creativity and curiosity. Creativity helps generate new ideas for qualitative inquiry to capture changing or previously unknown realities. Curiosity provides scholars with an intense impetus for striving to interpret the unknown in their understanding of complexity and ambiguity.

Creative writing

Qualitative data narratives, at their best, create compelling stories and raise provocative questions. When an interesting and accomplished qualitative study is reported imaginatively, it should seduce readers, engaging them with the text much as might a good novel (Bansal & Corley, 2012). The proximity between qualitative research and the world of literary fiction frees researchers from rigid frameworks, allowing them to explore new possibilities in research practice. Thus, by embracing creative writing, researchers take readers on a journey (Berends & Deken, 2021). To do so, it is important to guide the readers' sensemaking in communicating what the research has to report about the world under scrutiny and the way that it is apprehended theoretically (Johanson, 2007).

Our book was inspired, in part, by the potential of writing to engage readers in situations, emotions, politics, paradoxes and plots unfolding through actors and actants. The point is to see the world differently, to question what has previously been tacitly taken for granted, to 'make problematic' (Blum, 1971). It is because realities, their informal as well as formal rules and devices, may be assumed to be unproblematic by those that use them, that inquiry cannot assume that simply *questioning* actors will reveal the practices in question. Interviews are a fieldwork method but not the only one; indeed, they are a very limited method. If you want to collect accounts responding to prepared questions, while they may be useful, the data will be limited to what people think they should say in response to these scripted questions. Far better to catch them unawares, in their everyday lives, observing its many scenes, recording it in as much detail as possible, attending to naturally occurring conversations, encounters and the mundane materiality of their daily life. Practices such as ethnomethodology, anthropological 'thick description' and analysis of actor networks can alert one to the complexity of the mundane world. Communicating this complexity takes the skills of a writer.

Creative writing may seem distant from the world of researchers trained in well-defined research protocols, specific techniques for collecting and analysing data, as well as frameworks for the presentation and discussion of their findings. However, this distance is smaller than imagined since "academics do what creative writers do: They create, discover, and try to bring to life both the individual and the unique" (Vickers, 2015, p. 82). Creative writing is deeply immersed in the world that it creates, using imagination to distil from situations and experiences of them whatever is needed to 'make problematic' (Vickers, 2013). Scholars can benefit from the varied types of creative writing to explore new paths with their qualitative investigations.

Lessons and tips

- There are various approaches researchers can use to develop qualitative investigations, such as narrative fiction, narrative (semi-) fiction and ethnographic fiction. These styles of creative writing open room for analysing humour, emotions, aesthetics and ambiguity of practices in all their politics and paradoxes.
- Creative writing communicates understanding of dynamics as they are gleaned methodologically. Using this approach, researchers can bring to life the phenomena under analysis and direct attention to matters that might otherwise remain unappreciated.

- By combining facts and fiction, narrative provides a remarkable strategy to create a story, one leading readers on a journey of discovery, engaging them with the text and making sense anew of the experiences researched.

Accessing fieldwork

Accessing fieldwork is a challenging process for qualitative researchers. Aiming to shed light on important issues of this process, we brought to life insights, issues and strategies for scholars seeking to negotiate access. Unlike many quantitative investigations, in which data is available in databases, qualitative inquiry requires direct contact with fieldwork situations and immersion for periods ranging from several weeks, sometimes months, to even years, so that the researcher can conduct interviews, make observations, record data either using audio or video as well as collect documents and access existing audiovisual materials. For subjects being researched, your doing these things can be demanding of their time and attention. Thus, to negotiate access, the researcher must consider the commitments entailed, the types of relationship established with research subjects, codes of ethics and protection of anonymity as well as what will be done with the data collected in fieldwork.

The researcher will have to negotiate with numerous agencies controlling fieldwork access. Seeking to access the fieldwork, researchers should consider different agencies and understand how research interlocutors relate to the contexts they enter (Aroles, 2020). Researchers need a story that is of interest and is understandable by lay persons that do not have scientific appreciation of issues that interest the researcher. To do this well, the researcher needs to be genuinely interested in the situations that they wish to investigate and to be able to talk about them in creative ways that engage lay interests. Always secure a formal contract allowing access in advance because reliance on informal contacts can collapse if that person leaves the scene, for whatever reasons. Negotiating and maintaining access is influenced by the social context being studied because access is a political, dynamic, fluid and temporal process that need to be (re)negotiated continually (Cunliffe & Alcadipani, 2016).

Lessons and tips

- Negotiating access is not an easy task. There are challenges that need to be overcome. To deal with these challenges, the researcher should act reciprocally with subjects and be sensitive about informal codes governing fieldwork access.

- Having access to fieldwork requires reflexive work by researchers, which considers commitments, subjects and socio-material elements involved in the research and fieldwork processes.
- Access challenges can lead research to insights and socio-material data. Challenges do not necessarily block access; they just demand that the researcher becomes more creative in knowing their story and telling it well. It is important to be attentive to heterogeneous data (e.g., websites or documents) that open new possibilities to start the fieldwork.

Reviewing the literature

Starting a new research project usually requires an initial mapping of the literatures of the field that the researcher assumes will inform their inquiry. The great thing about doing empirical research is that what you thought to be the case at the outset may change because of fieldwork, or encounters with other scholars, or ideas found in a new article or book. Events can change bearings.

Researchers, especially early career researchers, may find reviewing the literature difficult. A common question is: where do I start? Although the literature review may seem like an easy endeavour, as its main task is 'only' to read papers and books, it should be seen as an iterative procedure. As a researcher, you will have developed preferences for your theoretical sensemaking, favouring those texts that serve as personal exemplars that help you make sense of data that proves difficult, recalcitrant to analysis or not useful. The job of the researcher is to make whatever is at hand or becomes available something interesting.

For those drowning in the vast range of academic papers and books available in libraries and online, we presented an empirical method that allows researchers to find a good starting point and write their literature reviews. To do so, we provided a guide to gaining insights from exemplary publications and seminal authors. Following such a path offers direction for researchers to gather scattered knowledge about a topic and integrate creatively. Post, Sarala, Gatrell and Prescott (2020, p. 372) highlight that "a review that contributes to theory should stimulate readers to think differently about their future research, having gained new insights from the review". So, our purpose was to stimulate researchers to take seriously the task of developing theory through a literature review as a way scholars can produce knowledge (Jones & Gatrell, 2014).

The literature review is not an event but a process. When researchers enter fieldwork, irrespective of the theories that they approach it with, they will need constantly to be engaged in a dialectical struggle relating their library knowledge to their fieldwork experiences. Sometimes it will feel as if reconciling what you read with what you see and hear is tearing you in two, as others' ideas encountered in journals and books and your fieldwork experiences seem distant things. When this happens, keep reading, search out different things, use Google Scholar and your imagination. When using Google Scholar, think of the themes that are emergent from the field. List several different ways of expressing these themes. Then set the parameters of the Google Scholar search as the present year. Enter the themes decided on into Google Scholar in 'inverted commas' and see what comes up. If nothing much useful and interesting appears, extend the search back a year at a time progressively; maybe rethink the terms. Are there some authors that seem to be more heavily cited than others? Read their papers – not deeply but scan them. First, the abstract; if that seems relevant, check out the introduction. If that grabs your attention, look at the conclusions. If the conclusions seem useful, then put the paper to one side to reach for when you have completed your search. Repeat often.

Doing this Google Scholar search in this way means that you are not making the mistake of thinking that a literature review necessarily precedes and stops before accessing the field. The dialectic of reconciling fieldwork experiences with theoretical modes of thinking may be used to advance and develop theorizing. Theorizing as a gerund, an active verb, signif a process rather than meeting an a priori frame into which data can be stuffed. Theorizing, whether it is speculating and producing initial insights or creating models and explaining a phenomenon (Breslin & Gatrell, 2020), is what researchers must do if they are not to be just descriptive reporters. Good descriptive work, such as the account of carnival or disability teaching in the previous chapters, are necessary but more important are the questions with which we left the reader: what helps us understand what is described? How do we go from data, its depiction and representation, to theorizing? How do we 'make problematic'?

Lessons and tips

- Reviewing the literature is a demanding task of searching texts, scanning them to identify those suitable to the research aim and reading critically.
- Reviewing the literature is a process not an event; finding exemplars that can help you go on is an important part of the process of research. Once you have done that you know with whom you are having conversations as you 'make problematic'.
- Exemplary publications are signposts researchers can use to review the literature; they provide theoretical and methodological guides for unfamiliar situations.
- It is helpful to analyse exemplary publications' statements carefully as well as discussions of these in secondary literature that the researcher reviews. By using the notion of modalities, researchers can identify which statements deny, affirm, relate to or associate with the exemplary publication under analysis.

Collecting and analysing data

Collecting data is critical for any empirical research. Without data, there is nothing to discover, question or advance in theorizing but without analysis, researchers have only a disorganized dataset that can hardly communicate anything intelligible to the reader. Some qualitative empirical researchers investigate interesting and relevant topics but do not provide interesting and relevant reports. There are two main reasons why this the case. First, a poorly designed data collection protocol that does not meet the research goals or creates difficulties for the researcher in knowing what data to collect and how to do so. A key consideration is thinking beyond interviews, as we have said. Interview accounts are useful but are only 'accounts'. What is said and what is done in practice need not align any more than will different accounts of ostensibly the same phenomena or situation. Researchers that rely only on interview data are being both unduly reliant on easy data and blind to other opportunities for imaginatively accessing better data. Situational experiences are alive with data and researchers need to be aware of this teeming life. The second reason is that after collecting data, there is often a failure to ask the question, what do I do with it? There can be the tendency just to 'report' accounts. Doing this displays a lack of rigour in analysing data. Data needs to be deconstructed and reconstructed anew, using theorizing to do so, making it problematic. Analysing data is a task that requires great effort and discipline from researchers. Even with a good database, qualitative reports may fall short.

Aiming to help researchers, we developed guidelines for collecting and analysing data, offering directions to qualitative research for readers. The guidelines are based on the cartography of controversies. This approach is useful for inquiry into any topic marked by disagreements and conflicts between actors who start to question what was taken for granted (Venturini, 2010; Venturini & Munk, 2021). A lack of controversy in life exists only in the dreams and schemes of those gullible enough to believe that everyone should be 'on the same page', 'sharing common values', being a 'harmonious team'. An absence of controversy signifies complacency and a lack of innovation. Acknowledging that many researchers are anxious about controversies that they might encounter before and during data collection and analysis processes, we detailed how to conduct this task. The guidelines developed offer direction for a crucial stage of qualitative research and resolve common problems that researchers face in collecting and analysing data.

Lessons and tips

- Cartography of controversy is an important tool for collecting and analysing data that focuses on disagreements and conflicts between actors questioning taken-for-granted practices.
- To collect data on controversies, it is important to know what they are and differentiate them from a one-off conflict. Furthermore, researchers should be aware of the four criteria that are useful in choosing good controversies and be attentive to the five focal points that can ground protocols for collecting data in fieldwork.
- Data analysis based on the five focal points covers controversy dynamics and enables visual representations of the issues under analysis. The visual representations are essential to facilitate story making through creative writing.

Writing reports

Qualitative researchers spend much of their time doing fieldwork, observing people, interviewing subjects and collecting documents. They also spend long hours reading papers and books. Nevertheless, writing is often a neglected part of academic work, often not thought about too much, even though "our identities and reputations as academics are largely formed on the basis of what and how we write" (Cloutier, 2016, p. 69). While there are many approaches to writing, it should be good writing that is elegant to read, aesthetically pleasing in style and punctilious in grammar. Creative writing styles allow researchers to use creativity and imagination in producing a research report that is persuasive, compelling and engaging (Vickers, 2013).

Strict writing rules and explanations of how researchers write texts are not easy to establish in an acontextual way (Barley, 2006). Context, audience and purpose are essential to style. In this book, we invited researchers to open their minds to new writing styles, such as creative writing. Its value as a writing style is that can bring to the surface life's underlying realities in all their ambiguity and contextuality. Writing is a practice like any other. So, to master this practice, the researcher needs to perform it daily, trying out different styles to find one most suitable for the project at hand. The stories in this shortform book can motivate the reader to begin creative writing to enliven qualitative research reports imaginatively.

Lessons and tips

- Every research report is written to be read. So, when writing a qualitative report, researchers must consider carefully the role of readers. Readers hope to find a text that tells a plausible story, helps them make sense of the world and change their view about what was previously taken for granted.
- Creative writing can deliver a report that is engaging and enjoyable for readers, enacting stories that combine data and theory in writing that describes salient issues. Readers become participants in knowledge building as they read possibilities into what is written.
- Creative writing puts the reader at the researcher's side as they are led on a journey that started with the subjects' doings and accounts that were encountered and experienced during fieldwork. Readers may encounter research challenges, obstacles and disappointments, as well as enlightenment.

Final considerations

We hope our book can inspire researchers, scholars and students to engage in qualitative research with open minds and design their investigation creatively. We offer alternative styles of creative writing for this purpose. We do not intend to restrict options; there are many possibilities available that are helpful in facilitating access, writing a literature review, developing theorizing, improving collection and analysis of data. Researchers can and should combine them, when necessary, aware of the challenges of using novel methods while maintaining rigour.

One interesting initiative is the co-creation of knowledge. Co-creation is an attempt to bridge the research–practice gap through the direct involvement of subjects in fieldwork contexts in academic investigations (Sharma & Bansal, 2020a). Connecting the different knowledge backgrounds and finding points of intersection between researchers and practitioners is a fruitful endeavour in creating knowledge (Sharma & Bansal, 2020b). As presented in this book, creative writing may be a powerful tool to support the goal of research findings that are more impactful and relevant, motivating readers to make sense of the world around them and change their views of what is taken-for-granted.

Active practicing

Starting from the lessons and tips we provide in this final chapter, let us put the book's tools, ideas and recommendations into practice. To do so, we invite you to enact qualitative research. It does not have to be extensive research. Our goal is only to have you practice the lessons gleaned from each of the book's chapters. The fieldwork site can be in situ or online. The activity is divided into five parts. For each part, please do the following.

1   Write a short text pointing out the main characteristics of qualitative research and indicate its advantages in the face of the grand challenges that society and organizations face nowadays. Use the introduction chapter as a starting point for your text (500 words).
2   Choose a topic involving fieldwork. Before negotiating access, think reflectively and briefly write down the main ethical issues involved in the research. Afterwards, start the negotiation process to carry out fieldwork. Describe the challenges you might face during the process of negotiating access. Also, highlight any insights that popped into your mind that could point to research insights and

other types of data you had not thought of before (500 words). Use Chapter 1 as a starting point.

3   Write a literature review of the research topic you have chosen. Focus on the main concepts you will use to ground your study. Draw on the notion of exemplary publication to guide your literature review. Use Chapter 2 as a starting point (800 words).

4   Develop a protocol for collecting data. Apply and adapt (if necessary) the cartography of controversies protocol on your chosen topic. Try to collect data from various sources, such as field notes, interviews and documents. The fieldwork does not need to be extensive. A few hours of observations, a few interviews and documents are enough for our goal of putting learning into practice. As you collect data, start the analysis. Do not wait to start the analysis until only after you have collected all the data. At this stage, consider the controversy analysis process presented in the book. Remember: this process is flexible. You can and should adapt it to your research topic as needed. Use Chapter 3 as a starting point (1,000–3,000 words).

5   Present your findings based on any style of creative writing, such as autoethnography or narrative (semi-)fiction. Use your imagination and creativity to provide a compelling story that captures the readers' attention and engages them with the text. Do not forget to bring the emotionality, politicality, paradoxicality, ambiguity and complexity of everyday life to the surface of the text. Use Chapter 4 as a starting point (2,000–4,000 words).

References

Aroles, J. (2020). Ethnographic encounters: Towards a minor politics of field access. *Culture and Organization*, 26(1), 48–60.

Bansal, P. & Corley, K. (2012). What's different about qualitative? *Academy of Management Journal*, 55(3), 509–513.

Barley, S. R. (2006). When I write my masterpiece: Thoughts on what makes a paper interesting. *Academy of Management Journal*, 49(1), 16–20.

Berends, H. & Deken, F. (2021) Composing qualitative process research. *Strategic Organization*, 19(1), 1–13.

Blum, A. F. (1971). Theorizing. In Douglas, J. D. (Ed.) *Understanding everyday life: Towards the reconstruction of sociological knowledge* (pp. 301–331). London: Routledge & Keagan Paul.

Breslin, D. & Gatrell, C. (2020). Theorizing through literature reviews: The miner-prospector continuum. *Organizational Research Methods*, Online first.https://journals.sagepub.com/doi/full/10.1177/1094428120943288

Cloutier, C. (2016). How I write: An inquiry into the writing practices of academics. *Journal of Management Inquiry*, 25(1) 69–84.

Cunliffe, A. L. & Alcadipani, R. (2016). The politics of access in fieldwork: Immersion, backstage dramas, and deception. *Organizational Research Methods*, 19(4), 535–561.

Eisenhardt, K. M., Graebner, M. E. & Sonenshein S. (2016). Grand challenges and inductive methods: Rigor without rigor mortis. *Academy of Management Journal*, 59(4), 1113–1123.

Johanson, L. M. (2007). Sitting in your reader's chair attending to your academic sensemakers. *Journal of Management Inquiry*, 16(3), 290–294.

Jones, O. & Gatrell, C. (2014). The future of writing and reviewing for IJMR. *International Journal of Management Reviews*, 16(3), 249–264.

Mills, C. W. (2000). *The sociological imagination.* Oxford: Oxford University Press.

Post, C., Sarala, R., Gatrell, C. & Prescott, J. E. (2020). Advancing theory with review articles. *Journal of Management Studies*, 57(2), 351–376.

Sharma, G. & Bansal, P. (2020a). Cocreating rigorous and relevant knowledge. *Academy of Management Journal*, 63(2), 386–410.

Sharma, G., & Bansal, P. (2020b). Partnering up: Including managers as research partners in systematic reviews. *Organizational Research Methods*, Online first. https://journals.sagepub.com/doi/abs/10.1177/1094428120965706

Venturini, T. (2010). Diving in magma: How to explore controversies with actor-network theory, public. *Understanding of Science*, 19(3): 258–273.

Venturini, T. & Munk, A. K. (2021). *Controversy mapping: A field guide.* London: Polity.

Vickers, M. H. (2013). Three stories—and a writer's tale: A creative writing case study of workplace bullying. *Organization Management Journal*, 10, 139–147.

Vickers, M. H. (2015). Stories, disability, and "dirty" workers: Creative writing to go beyond too few words. *Journal of Management Inquiry*, 24(1), 82–89.

Index

Printed in the United States
by Baker & Taylor Publisher Services